HAPPINESS HOMEMADE

HAPPINESS HOMEMADE

BY ELLEN G. WHITE

Southern Publishing Association
Nashville, Tennessee

Copyright © 1971 by
Southern Publishing Association
Library of Congress
Catalog Card No. 70-173421
SBN 8127-0056-2

Abridged from THE ADVENTIST HOME
Copyright © 1952 by
Ellen G. White Publications

This book was:
Designed by Dean Tucker
Cover art and illustrations
by Ralph McDonald
Text set in 11/13 Fairfield
Printed on Lock Haven Antique
Cover stock: Springhill Gloss Bristol C1S

Printed in U.S.A.

FOREWORD

Never in the history of the world has a book like HAPPINESS HOMEMADE been needed more urgently than right now. Never have parents and children been more anxious for the right answers to their everyday problems. Never have more homes been in such jeopardy as they are today.

Everyone knows that conditions in society are but a reflection of conditions in the homes of our nation. We also know that changes in our homes will be mirrored in a changed society. To this end HAPPINESS HOMEMADE has been dedicated.

The author, Ellen G. White, the mother of four sons and a religious writer with deep insights, has presented much valuable counsel for parents and children. In so doing she has touched on almost every phase of the home and family life. She offers helpful guidance on many of the problems that give great concern to thoughtful and anxious parents today.

The materials comprising this volume appeared first in numerous published articles, book chapters, and correspondence with parents. That which is presented in this compact form is selected from a more comprehensive popular work on the Christian home issued by this publisher.

THE PUBLISHERS

CONTENTS

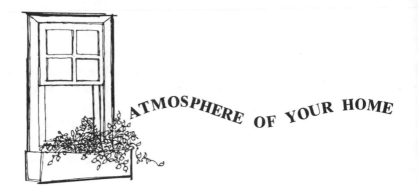

ATMOSPHERE OF YOUR HOME

Home, the Foundation of Society: Society is composed of families, and is what the heads of families make it. Out of the heart are "the issues of life"; and the heart of the community, of the church, and of the nation is the household. The well-being of society, the success of the church, the prosperity of the nation, depend upon home influences.

The elevation or deterioration of the future of society will be determined by the manners and morals of the youth growing up around us. As the youth are educated, and as their characters are molded in their childhood to virtuous habits, self-control, and temperance, so will their influence be upon society. If they are left unenlightened and uncontrolled, and as the result become self-willed, intemperate in appetite and passion, so will be their future influence in molding society. The company which the young now keep, the habits they now form, and the principles they now adopt are the index to the state of society for years to come.

Bit of Heaven on Earth: Home should be made all that the word implies. It should be a little heaven upon earth, a place where the affections are cultivated instead of being studiously repressed. Our happiness depends upon this cultivation of love, sympathy, and true courtesy to one another.

9

To a large extent parents create the atmosphere of the home circle, and when there is disagreement between father and mother, the children partake of the same spirit. Make your home atmosphere fragrant with tender thoughtfulness. If you have become estranged and have failed to be Bible Christians, be converted. If you would be a saint in heaven, you must first be a saint on earth. The traits of character you cherish in life will not be changed by death or by the resurrection. You will come up from the grave with the same disposition you manifested in your home and in society. Jesus does not change the character at His coming. The work of transformation must be done now. Our daily lives are determining our destiny.

Importance of Rules: Every Christian home should have rules; and parents should, in their words and deportment toward each other, give to the children a precious, living example of what they desire them to be. Purity in speech and true Christian courtesy should be constantly practiced. Teach the children and youth to respect themselves, to be true to God, true to principle; teach them to respect and obey the law of God.

These principles will control their lives and will be carried out in their associations with others. They will create a pure atmosphere—one that will have an influence that will encourage weak souls in the upward path that leads to holiness and heaven. Let every lesson be of an elevating and ennobling character, and the records made in the books of heaven will be such as you will not be ashamed to meet in the judgment.

Children who receive this kind of instruction will be prepared to fill places of responsibility and, by precept and example, will be constantly aiding others to do right. Those whose moral sensibilities have not been blunted will appreciate right principles; they will put a just estimate upon their natural endowments and will make the best use of their physical, mental, and moral powers. Such souls are strongly fortified against temptation; they are surrounded by a wall not easily broken down.

Make Home Bright and Happy: Troubles may invade, but these are the lot of humanity. Let patience, gratitude, and love keep sunshine in the heart though the day may be ever so cloudy.

The home may be plain, but it can always be a place where cheerful words are spoken and kindly deeds are done, where courtesy and love are abiding guests.

Administer the rules of the home in wisdom and love, not with a rod of iron. Children will respond with willing obedience to the rule of love. Commend your children whenever you can. Make their lives as happy as possible. Keep the soil of the heart mellow by the manifestation of love and affection, thus preparing it for the seed of truth. Remember that the Lord gives the earth not only clouds and rain, but the beautiful, smiling sunshine, causing the seed to germinate and the blossom to appear. Remember that children need not only reproof and correction, but encouragement and commendation, the pleasant sunshine of kind words.

Christ's Presence: The home that is beautified by love, sympathy, and tenderness is a place that angels love to visit, and where God is glorified. The influence of a carefully guarded Christian home in the years of childhood and youth is the surest safeguard against corruption. In the atmosphere of such a home the children will learn to love both their earthly parents and their heavenly Father.

Holiness to God is to pervade the home. Parents and children are to educate themselves to cooperate with God. They are to bring their habits and practices into harmony with God's plans.

The family relationship should be sanctifying in its influence. Christian homes, established and conducted in accordance with God's plan, are a wonderful help in forming Christian character. Parents and children should unite in offering loving service to Him who alone can keep human love pure and noble.

FUNDAMENTALS OF TRUE HOMEMAKING

Attractive Homes Needed: While there are weighty responsibilities devolving upon the parents to guard carefully the future happiness and interests of their children, it is also their duty to make home as attractive as possible. This is of far greater consequence than to acquire estates and money. Home must not lack sunshine. The home feeling should be kept alive in the hearts of the children, that they may look back upon the home of their childhood as a place of peace and happiness next to heaven. Then as they come to maturity, they should in their turn try to be a comfort and blessing to their parents.

The home should be to the children the most attractive place in the world, and the mother's presence should be its greatest attraction. Children have sensitive, loving natures. They are easily pleased, and easily made unhappy. By gentle discipline, in loving words and acts, mothers may bind their children to their hearts.

Clean, Neat, Orderly: Cleanliness, neatness, and order are indispensable to the proper management of the household. But when the mother makes these the all-important duties of her life, and devotes herself to them, to the neglect of the physical development and the mental and moral training of her children, she makes a sad mistake.

While we are to guard against needless adornment and display, we are in no case to be careless and indifferent in regard to outward appearance. All about our persons and our homes is to be neat and attractive. The youth are to be taught the importance of presenting an appearance above criticism, an appearance that honors God and the truth.

God is displeased with disorder, slackness, and a lack of thoroughness in anyone. These deficiencies are serious evils, and tend to wean the affections of the husband from the wife when the husband loves order, well-disciplined children, and a well-regulated house. A wife and mother cannot make home agreeable and happy unless she possesses a love for order, preserves her dignity, and has good government; therefore all who fail on these points should begin at once to educate themselves in this direction, and cultivate the very things wherein is their greatest lack.

Everyday Tasks: All the work we do that is necessary to be done, be it washing dishes, setting tables, waiting upon the sick, cooking, or washing, is of moral importance. The humble tasks before us are to be taken up by someone; and those who do them should feel that they are doing a necessary and honorable work, and that in their mission, humble though it may be, they are doing the work of God just as surely as was Gabriel when sent to the prophets.

MAN'S FIRST HOME

Prepared by God: The Eden home of our first parents was prepared for them by God Himself. When He had furnished it with everything that man could desire, He said, "Let us make man in our image, after our likeness."

The Lord was pleased with this last and noblest of all His creatures, and designed that he should be the perfect inhabitant of a perfect world. But it was not His purpose that man should live in solitude. He said, "It is not good that the man should be alone; I will make him an help meet for him."

God Himself gave Adam a companion. He provided "an help meet for him"—a helper corresponding to him—one who was fitted to be his companion, and who could be one with him in love and sympathy.

Eve was created from a rib taken from the side of Adam, signifying that she was not to control him as the head, nor to be trampled under his feet as an inferior, but to stand by his side as an equal, to be loved and protected by him. A part of man, bone of his bone, and flesh of his flesh, she was his second self; showing the close union and the affectionate attachment that should exist in this relation. "For no man ever yet hated his own flesh; but nourisheth and cherisheth it." "Therefore shall a man leave his father and his mother, and shall cleave unto his wife: and they shall be one."

The First Marriage: God celebrated the first marriage. Thus the institution has for its originator the Creator of the universe. "Marriage is honourable"; it was one of the first gifts of God to man, and it is one of the two institutions that, after the fall, Adam brought with him beyond the gates of Paradise. When the divine principles are recognized and obeyed in this relation, marriage is a blessing; it guards the purity and happiness of the race, it provides for man's social needs, it elevates the physical, the intellectual, and the moral nature.

Every Want Supplied: Adam was surrounded with everything his heart could wish. Every want was supplied. There were no sin and no signs of decay in glorious Eden. Angels of God conversed freely and lovingly with the holy pair. The happy songsters caroled forth their free, joyous songs of praise to their Creator. The peaceful beasts in happy innocence played about Adam and Eve, obedient to their word. Adam was in the perfection of manhood, the noblest of the Creator's work.

15

To Adam was given the work of caring for the garden. The Creator knew that Adam could not be happy without employment. The beauty of the garden delighted him, but this was not enough. He must have labor to call into exercise the wonderful organs of the body. Had happiness consisted in doing nothing, man, in his state of holy innocence, would have been left unemployed. But He who created man knew what would be for his happiness; and no sooner had He created him than He gave him his appointed work. The promise of future glory, and the decree that man must toil for his daily bread, came from the same throne.

Honor God: Fathers and mothers who make God first in their households, who teach their children that the fear of the Lord is the beginning of wisdom, glorify God before angels and before men by presenting a well-ordered, well-disciplined family —a family that love and obey God instead of rebelling against Him. Christ is not a stranger in their homes; His name is a household name, revered and glorified.

Angels delight in a home where God reigns supreme and the children are taught to reverence religion, the Bible, and their Creator. Such families can claim the promise, "Them that honour me I will honour." As from such a home the father goes forth to his daily duties, it is with a spirit softened and subdued by converse with God.

INFLUENCE
OF YOUR HOME

An Object Lesson: The home in which the members are polite, courteous Christians exerts a far-reaching influence for good. Other families will mark the results attained by such a home, and will follow the example set, in their turn guarding the home against satanic influences.

One well-ordered, well-disciplined family tells more in behalf of Christianity than all the sermons that can be preached. Such a family gives evidence that the parents have been successful in following God's directions, and that their children will serve Him in the church. Their influence grows; for as they impart, they receive to impart again.

The father and mother find helpers in their children, who give to others the instruction received in the home. The neighborhood in which they live is helped, for in it they have become enriched for time and for eternity. The whole family is engaged in the service of the Master; and by their godly example, others are inspired to be faithful and true to God in dealing with His flock, His beautiful flock.

Wonderful Possibilities: Our time here is short. We can pass through this world but once; as we pass along, let us make the most of life. The work to which we are called does not require wealth or social position or great ability. It requires a kindly, self-sacrificing spirit and a steadfast purpose. A lamp, however small, if kept steadily burning, may be the means of lighting many other lamps. Our sphere of influence may seem narrow, our ability small, our opportunities few, our acquirements limited; yet wonderful possibilities are ours through a faithful use of the opportunities of our own homes. If we will open our hearts and homes to the divine principles of life, we shall become channels for currents of life-giving power. From our homes will flow streams of healing, bringing life, and beauty, and fruitfulness where now are barrenness and dearth.

It is impossible for any of us to live in such a way that we shall not cast an influence in the world. No member of the family can enclose himself within himself, where other members of the family shall not feel his influence and spirit. The very expression of the countenance has an influence for good or evil.

The influence of an ill-regulated family is widespread, and disastrous to all society. It accumulates in a tide of evil that affects families, communities, and governments.

A Powerful Argument: When our own homes are what they should be, our children will not be allowed to grow up in idleness and indifference to the claims of God in behalf of the needy all about them. As the Lord's heritage, they will be qualified to take up the work where they are. A light will shine from such homes which will reveal itself in behalf of the ignorant, leading them to the source of all knowledge. An influence will be exerted that will be a power for God and for His truth.

Cheerful Homes Influence Neighbors: We need more sunshiny parents and more sunshiny Christians. We are too much shut up within ourselves. Too often the kindly, encouraging word, the cheery smile, are withheld from our children and from the oppressed and discouraged.

Results of Family Unity: The first work of Christians is to be united in the family. Then the work is to extend to their neighbors nigh and afar off. Their words, fragrant with the love of Christ, are to be a savor of life unto life.

The more closely the members of a family are united in their work in the home, the more uplifting and helpful will be the influence that father and mother and sons and daughters will exert outside the home.

Good Men Needed: The happiness of families and churches depends upon home influences. Eternal interests depend upon the proper discharge of the duties of this life. The world is not so much in need of great minds as of good men who will be a blessing in their homes.

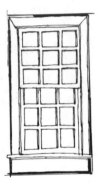

God's Purpose for the Husband and Wife: God made from the man a woman, to be a companion and helpmeet for him, to be one with him, to cheer, encourage, and bless him, he in his turn to be her strong helper. All who enter into matrimonial relations with a holy purpose—the husband to obtain the pure affections of a woman's heart, the wife to soften and improve her husband's character and give it completeness—fulfill God's purpose for them.

Christ came not to destroy this institution, but to restore it to its original sanctity and elevation. He came to restore the moral image of God in man, and He began His work by sanctioning the marriage relation.

The divine love emanating from Christ never destroys human love, but includes it. By it human love is refined and purified, elevated and ennobled. Human love can never bear its precious fruit until it is united with the divine nature and trained to grow heavenward. Jesus wants to see happy marriages, happy firesides.

Like every other one of God's good gifts entrusted to the keeping of humanity, marriage has been perverted by sin; but it is the purpose of the gospel to restore its purity and beauty.

The grace of Christ, and this alone, can make this institution what God designed it should be—an agent for the blessing and uplifting of humanity. And thus the families of earth, in their unity and peace and love, may represent the family of heaven.

A Joyous Occasion: The Scriptures state that both Jesus and His disciples were called to this marriage feast [at Cana]. Christ has given Christians no sanction to say when invited to a marriage, "We ought not to be present on so joyous an occasion." By attending this feast Christ taught that He would have us rejoice with those who do rejoice in the observance of His statutes. He never discouraged the innocent festivities of mankind when carried on in accordance with the laws of Heaven.

The Blending of Two Lives: If the contracting parties are agreed in religious belief and practice, and everything is consistent, marriage at this time need not be displeasing to God.

In the marriage relation there is a very important step taken —the blending of two lives into one.

The blessing of God in the home where this union shall exist is as the sunshine of heaven, because it is the Lord's ordained will that man and wife should be linked together in holy bonds of union, under Jesus Christ, with Him to control, and His Spirit to guide.

God wants the home to be the happiest place on earth, the very symbol of the home in heaven. Bearing the marriage responsibilities in the home, linking their interests with Jesus Christ, leaning upon His arm and His assurance, husband and wife may share a happiness in this union that angels of God commend.

Counsel to the Newly Married Pair: You have united in a lifelong covenant. Your education in married life has begun. The first year of married life is a year of experience, a year in which husband and wife learn each other's different traits of character, as a child learns lessons in school. In this, the first year of your married life, let there be no chapters that will mar your future happiness.

In your life union your affections are to be tributary to each other's happiness. Each is to minister to the happiness of the other. This is the will of God concerning you. But while you are to blend as one, neither of you is to lose his or her individuality in the other. God is the owner of your individuality. Of Him you are to ask: What is right? What is wrong? How may I best fulfill the purpose of my creation?

A Pledge Before Heavenly Witnesses: God has ordained that there should be perfect love and harmony between those who enter into the marriage relation. Let bride and bridegroom, in the presence of the heavenly universe, pledge themselves to love each other as God has ordained they should. The wife is to respect and reverence her husband, and the husband is to love and cherish his wife.

Men and women, at the beginning of married life, should reconsecrate themselves to God.

A HAPPY, SUCCESSFUL PARTNERSHIP

A Lifelong Experience: To gain a proper understanding of the marriage relation is the work of a lifetime. Those who marry enter a school from which they are never in this life to be graduated.

However carefully and wisely marriage may have been entered into, few couples are completely united when the marriage ceremony is performed. The real union of the two in wedlock is the work of the afteryears.

As life with its burden of perplexity and care meets the newly wedded pair, the romance with which imagination so often invests marriage disappears. Husband and wife learn each other's character as it was impossible to learn it in their previous association. This is a most critical period in their experience. The happiness and usefulness of their whole future life depend upon their taking a right course now. Often they discern in each other unsuspected weaknesses and defects; but the hearts that love has united will discern excellencies also heretofore unknown. Let all seek to discover the excellencies rather than the defects. Often it is our own attitude, the atmosphere that surrounds ourselves, which determines what will be revealed to us in another.

Love Must Grow: Affection may be as clear as crystal and beauteous in its purity, yet it may be shallow because it has not been tested and tried. Make Christ first and last and best in everything. Constantly behold Him, and your love for Him will daily become deeper and stronger as it is submitted to the test of trial. And as your love for Him increases, your love for each other will grow deeper and stronger.

Though difficulties, perplexities, and discouragements may arise, let neither husband nor wife harbor the thought that their union is a mistake or a disappointment. Determine to be all that it is possible to be to each other. Continue the early attentions. In every way encourage each other in fighting the battles of life. Study to advance the happiness of each other. Let there be mutual love, mutual forbearance. Then marriage, instead of being the end of love, will be as it were the very beginning of love. The warmth of true friendship, the love that binds heart to heart, is a foretaste of the joys of heaven.

Counsel to a Strong-willed Couple: Neither husband nor wife is to make a plea for rulership. The Lord has laid down the principle that is to guide in this matter. The husband is to cherish his wife as Christ cherishes the church. And the wife is to respect and love her husband. Both are to cultivate the spirit of kindness, being determined never to grieve or injure the other.

Do not try to compel each other to do as you wish. You cannot do this and retain each other's love. Manifestations of self-will destroy the peace and happiness of the home. Let not your married life be one of contention. If you do, you will both be unhappy. Be kind in speech and gentle in action, giving up your own wishes. Watch well your words, for they have a powerful influence for good or for ill. Allow no sharpness to come into your voices. Bring into your united life the fragrance of Christlikeness.

Words and Deeds of Love: There are many who regard the expression of love as a weakness, and they maintain a reserve that repels others. This spirit checks the current of sympathy. As the social and generous impulses are repressed, they wither, and the heart becomes desolate and cold. We should beware of this error. Love cannot long exist without expression. Let not the heart of one connected with you starve for the want of kindness and sympathy.

Let each give love rather than exact it. Cultivate that which is noblest in yourselves, and be quick to recognize the good qualities in each other. The consciousness of being appreciated is a wonderful stimulus and satisfaction. Sympathy and respect encourage the striving after excellence, and love itself increases as it stimulates to nobler aims.

Characteristics of a Good Wife and Mother: Instead of sinking into a mere household drudge, let the wife and mother take time to read, to keep herself well informed, to be a companion to her husband, and to keep in touch with the developing minds of her children. Let her use wisely the opportunities now hers to influence her dear ones for the higher life. Let her take time to make the dear Saviour a daily Companion and familiar

Friend. Let her take time for the study of His Word, take time to go with the children into the fields and learn of God through the beauty of His works.

Let her keep cheerful and buoyant. Instead of spending every moment in endless sewing, make the evening a pleasant social season, a family reunion after the day's duties. Many a man would thus be led to choose the society of his home before that of the clubhouse. Many a boy would be kept from the street. Many a girl would be saved from frivolous, misleading associations. The influence of the home would be to parents and children what God designed it should be, a lifelong blessing.

Mutual Love and Forbearance Rewarded: Without mutual forbearance and love no earthly power can hold you and your husband in the bonds of Christian unity. Your companionship in the marriage relation should be close and tender, holy and elevated, breathing a spiritual power into your lives, that you may be everything to each other that God's Word requires. When you reach the condition that the Lord desires you to reach, you will find heaven below and God in your life.

Men and women can reach God's ideal for them if they will take Christ as their helper. What human wisdom cannot do, His grace will accomplish for those who give themselves to Him in loving trust. His providence can unite hearts in bonds that are of heavenly origin. Love will not be a mere exchange of soft and flattering words. The loom of heaven weaves with warp and woof finer, yet more firm, than can be woven by the looms of earth. The result is not a tissue fabric, but a texture that will bear wear and test and trial. Heart will be bound to heart in the golden bonds of a love that is enduring.

MUTUAL OBLIGATIONS

Each Has Responsibilities: The two who unite their interest in life will have distinct characteristics and individual responsibilities. Each one will have his or her work, but women are not to be valued by the amount of work they can do as are beasts of burden. The wife is to grace the family circle as a wife and companion to a wise husband. At every step she should inquire, "Is this the standard of true womanhood?" and, "How shall I make my influence Christlike in my home?" The husband should let his wife know that he appreciates her work.

27

The wife is to respect her husband. The husband is to love and cherish his wife; and as their marriage vow unites them as one, so their belief in Christ should make them one in Him. What can be more pleasing to God than to see those who enter into the marriage relation seek together to learn of Jesus and to become more and more imbued with His Spirit?

Wives Submit; Husbands Love: The question is often asked, "Shall a wife have no will of her own?" The Bible plainly states that the husband is the head of the family. "Wives, submit yourselves unto your own husbands." If this injunction ended here, we might say that the position of the wife is not an enviable one; it is a very hard and trying position in very many cases, and it would be better were there fewer marriages. Many husbands stop at the words, "Wives, submit yourselves," but we will read the conclusion of the same injunction, which is, "As it is fit in the Lord."

Mutual Forbearance: We must have the Spirit of God, or we can never have harmony in the home. The wife, if she has the spirit of Christ, will be careful of her words; she will control her spirit, she will be submissive, and yet will not feel that she is a bondslave, but a companion to her husband. If the husband is a servant of God, he will not lord it over his wife; he will not be arbitrary and exacting. We cannot cherish home affection with too much care; for the home, if the Spirit of the Lord dwells there, is a type of heaven. If one errs, the other will exercise Christlike forbearance and not draw coldly away.

Neither the husband nor the wife should attempt to exercise over the other an arbitrary control. Do not try to compel each other to yield to your wishes. You cannot do this and retain each other's love. Be kind, patient, and forbearing, considerate, and courteous. By the grace of God you can succeed in making each other happy, as in your marriage vow you promised to do.

Each to Graciously Yield: In the married life men and women sometimes act like undisciplined, perverse children. The husband wants his way, and the wife wants her way, and neither is willing to yield. Such a condition of things can bring only the greatest unhappiness. Both husband and wife should be willing to yield his or her way or opinion. There is no possibility of happiness while they both persist in doing as they please.

Unless men and women have learned of Christ, His meekness and lowliness, they will reveal the impulsive, unreasonable spirit so often revealed by children. The strong, undisciplined will will seek to rule. Such ones need to study the words of Paul: "When I was a child, I spake as a child, I understood as a child, I thought as a child: but when I became a man, I put away childish things."

Christ Brings Unity: If the will of God is fulfilled, the husband and wife will respect each other and cultivate love and confidence. Anything that would mar the peace and unity of the family should be firmly repressed, and kindness and love should be cherished. He who manifests the spirit of tenderness, forbearance, and love will find that the same spirit will be reflected upon him. Where the Spirit of God reigns, there will be no talk of unsuitability in the marriage relation. If Christ indeed is formed within, the hope of glory, there will be union and love in the home. Christ abiding in the heart of the wife will be at agreement with Christ abiding in the heart of the husband. They will be striving together for the mansions Christ has gone to prepare for those who love Him.

WHERE SHOULD YOUR HOME BE?

Choosing the Location: In choosing a home, God would have us consider, first of all, the moral and religious influences that will surround us and our families.

As the location for a home is sought, let this purpose direct the choice. Be not controlled by the desire for wealth, the dictates of fashion, or the customs of society. Consider what will tend most to simplicity, purity, health, and real worth.

Instead of dwelling where only the works of men can be seen, where the sights and sounds frequently suggest thoughts of evil, where turmoil and confusion bring weariness and disquietude, go where you can look upon the works of God. Find rest of spirit in the beauty and quietude and peace of nature. Let the eye rest on the green fields, the groves, and the hills. Look up to the blue sky, unobscured by the city's dust and smoke, and breathe the invigorating air of heaven.

Christ's Earthly Home: Jesus came to this earth to accomplish the greatest work ever accomplished among men. He came as

God's ambassador, to show us how to live so as to secure life's best results. What were the conditions chosen by the Infinite Father for His Son? A secluded home in the Galilean hills; a household sustained by honest, self-respecting labor; a life of simplicity; daily conflict with difficulty and hardship; self-sacrifice, economy, and patient, gladsome service; the hour of study at His mother's side, with the open scroll of Scripture; the quiet of dawn or twilight in the green valley; the holy ministries of nature; the study of creation and providence; and the soul's communion with God—these were the conditions and opportunities of the early life of Jesus.

Other Men Reared in Country Homes: So with the great majority of the best and noblest men of all ages. Read the history of Abraham, Jacob, and Joseph; of Moses, David, and Elisha. Study the lives of men of later times who have most worthily filled positions of trust and responsibility.

How many of these were reared in country homes! They knew little of luxury. They did not spend their youth in amusement.

Many were forced to struggle with poverty and hardship. They early learned to work, and their active life in the open air gave vigor and elasticity to all their faculties. Forced to depend upon their own resources, they learned to combat difficulties and to surmount obstacles, and they gained courage and perseverance. They learned the lessons of self-reliance and self-control. Sheltered in a great degree from evil associations, they were satisfied with natural pleasures and wholesome companionships. They were simple in their tastes and temperate in their habits. They were governed by principle, and they grew up pure and strong and true. When called to their lifework, they brought to it physical and mental power, buoyancy of spirit, ability to plan and execute, and steadfastness in resisting evil that made them a positive power for good in the world.

31

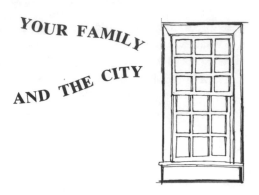

YOUR FAMILY AND THE CITY

Hazards of City Life: Life in the cities is false and artificial. The intense passion for money getting, the whirl of excitement and pleasure seeking, the thirst for display, the luxury and extravagance—all are forces that, with the great masses of mankind, are turning the mind from life's true purpose. They are opening the door to a thousand evils. Upon the youth they have almost irresistible power. One of the most subtle and dangerous temptations that assails the children and youth in the cities is the love of pleasure.

Consider Pollution: The physical surroundings in the cities are often a peril to health. The constant liability to contact with disease, the prevalence of foul air, impure water, impure food, the crowded, dark, unhealthful dwellings, are some of the many evils to be met.

It was not God's purpose that people should be crowded into cities, huddled together in terraces and tenements. In the beginning He placed our first parents amidst the beautiful sights and sounds He desires us to rejoice in today. The more nearly we come into harmony with God's original plan, the more favorable will be our position to secure health of body and mind and soul.

For Love of Gain: It is often the case that parents are not careful to surround their children with right influences. In choosing a home, they think more of their worldly interests than of the moral and social atmosphere, and the children form associations that are unfavorable to the development of piety and the formation of right characters.

Cities Offer No Real Benefit: There is not one family in a hundred who will be improved physically, mentally, or spiritually by residing in the city. Faith, hope, love, happiness, can far better be gained in retired places, where there are fields and hills and trees. Take your children away from the sights and sounds of the city, and their minds will become more healthy. It will be found easier to bring home to their hearts the truth of the Word of God.

Moving From Rural to City Areas: Many parents remove from their country homes to the city, regarding it as a more desirable or profitable location. But by making this change, they expose their children to many and great temptations. The boys have no employment, and they obtain a street education and go on from one step in depravity to another, until they lose all interest in anything that is good and pure and holy. How much better had the parents remained with their families in the country, where the influences are most favorable for physical and mental strength.

Better sacrifice any and every worldly consideration than to imperil the precious souls committed to your care. They will be assailed by temptations and should be taught to meet them; but it is your duty to cut off every influence, to break up every habit, to sunder every tie, that keeps you from the most free, open, and hearty committal of yourselves and your family to God.

Instead of the crowded city seek some retired situation where your children will be, so far as possible, shielded from temptation, and there train and educate them for usefulness.

BUILDING
AND FURNISHING
YOUR HOME

Ventilation, Sunlight, and Drainage: In the construction of buildings, whether for public purposes or as dwellings, care should be taken to provide for good ventilation and plenty of sunlight.

So far as possible, all buildings intended for human habitation should be placed on high, well-drained ground. This will ensure a dry site. This matter is often too lightly regarded. Continuous ill health, serious diseases, and many deaths result from low-lying, ill-drained situations.

In the building of houses it is especially important to secure thorough ventilation and plenty of sunlight. Let there be a current of air and an abundance of light in every room in the house. Sleeping rooms should be so arranged as to have a free circulation of air day and night. No room is fit to be occupied as a sleeping room unless it can be thrown open daily to the air and sunshine.

The Yard: A yard beautified with scattering trees and some

34

shrubbery, at a proper distance from the house, has a happy influence upon the family, and, if well taken care of, will prove no injury to the health. But shade trees and shrubbery close and dense around a house make it unhealthful, for they prevent the free circulation of air and shut out the rays of the sun.

The Effect of Natural Beauty on Your Household: God loves the beautiful. He has clothed the earth and the heavens with beauty, and with a Father's joy He watches the delight of His children in the things that He has made. He desires us to surround our homes with the beauty of natural things.

Nearly all dwellers in the country, however poor, could have about their homes a bit of grassy lawn, a few shade trees, flowering shrubbery, or fragrant blossoms. And far more than any artificial adorning will they minister to the happiness of the household. They will bring into the homelife a softening, refining influence, strengthening the love of nature and drawing the members of the household nearer to one another and nearer to God.

Simple Home Furnishings: Our artificial habits deprive us of many blessings and much enjoyment, and unfit us for living the most useful lives. Elaborate and expensive furnishings are a waste not only of money but of that which is a thousandfold more precious. They bring into the home a heavy burden of care and labor and perplexity.

Furnish your home with things plain and simple, things that will bear handling, that can be easily kept clean, and that can be replaced without great expense. By exercising taste, you can make a very simple home attractive and inviting, if love and contentment are there.

Being Too Neat: In some families there is too much done. Neatness and order are essential to comfort, but these virtues should not be carried to such an extreme as to make life a period of unceasing drudgery and to render the inmates of the home miserable. In the houses of some whom we highly esteem, there is a stiff precision about the arrangement of the furniture and belongings that is quite as disagreeable as a lack of order would be. The painful propriety which invests the whole house makes it impossible to find there that rest which one expects in the true home.

A Decorating Principle: The rigid precision which we have mentioned as being a disagreeable feature of so many homes is not in accordance with the great plan of nature. God has not caused the flowers of the fields to grow in regular beds, with set borders, but He has scattered them like gems over the greensward, and they beautify the earth with their variety of form and color. The trees of the forest are not in regular order. It is restful to eye and mind to range over the scenes of nature, over forest, hill, and valley, plain and river, enjoying the endless diversity of form and color, and the beauty with which trees, shrubs, and flowers are grouped in nature's garden, making it a picture of loveliness. Childhood, youth, and age can alike find rest and gratification there.

This law of variety can be in a measure carried out in the home. There should be a proper harmony of colors and a general fitness of things in the furnishing of a house; but it is not necessary to good taste that every article of furniture in a room should be of the same pattern in design, material, or upholstery; but, on the contrary, it is more pleasing to the eye that there should be a harmonious variety.

The very best part of the house, the sunniest and most inviting rooms, and the most comfortable furniture should be in a daily use by those who really live in the house. This will make home attractive to the inmates and also to that class of friends who really care for us, whom we could benefit, and by whom we could be benefited.

But whether the home be humble or elegant, its appointments costly or the reverse, there will be no happiness within its walls unless the spirit of its inmates is in harmony with the divine will. Contentment should reign within the household.

The Children's Comfort and Welfare: It does not require costly surroundings and expensive furniture to make children contented and happy in their homes, but it is necessary that the parents give them tender love and careful attention.

Don't say to them as I have heard many mothers say, "There is no room for you here in the parlor. Don't sit on that sofa that is covered with satin damask. We don't want you to sit down on that sofa." And when they go into another room, "We don't want your noise here." And they go into the kitchen, and the cook says, "I cannot be bothered with you here. Go out from here with your noise; you pester me so, and bother me." Where do they go to receive their education? Into the street.

More Precious Than Luxury: Too many cares and burdens are brought into our families, and too little of natural simplicity and peace and happiness is cherished. There should be less care for what the outside world will say, and more thoughtful attention to the members of the family circle. There should be less display and affectation of worldly politeness, and much more tenderness and love, cheerfulness and Christian courtesy, among the members of the household. Many need to learn how to make home attractive, a place of enjoyment. Thankful hearts and kind looks are more valuable than wealth and luxury, and contentment with simple things will make home happy if love be there.

Jesus, our Redeemer, walked the earth with the dignity of a king; yet He was meek and lowly of heart. He was a light and blessing in every home because He carried cheerfulness, hope, and courage with Him. Oh, that we could be satisfied with less heart longings, less striving for things difficult to obtain wherewith to beautify our homes, while that which God values above jewels, the meek and quiet spirit, is not cherished. The grace of simplicity, meekness, and true affection would make a paradise of the humblest home. It is better to endure cheerfully every inconvenience than to part with peace and contentment.

CHILDREN, A BLESSING

God Planned for Families: He who gave Eve to Adam as a helpmeet ordained that men and women should be united in holy wedlock, to rear families whose members, crowned with honor, should be recognized as members of the family above.

Children are the heritage of the Lord, and we are answerable to Him for our management of His property. In love, faith, and prayer let parents work for their households, until with joy they can come to God saying, "Behold, I and the children whom the Lord hath given me."

A childless house is a desolate place. The hearts of the inmates are in danger of becoming selfish, of cherishing a love for their own ease, and consulting their own desires and conveniences. They gather sympathy to themselves, but have little to bestow upon others.

Many are diseased physically, mentally, and morally because their attention is turned almost exclusively to themselves. They might be saved from stagnation by the healthy vitality of younger and varying minds and the restless energy of children.

Child-Caring Develops Character: The sympathy, forbearance, and love required in dealing with children would be a blessing in any household. They would soften and subdue set traits of character in those who need to be more cheerful and restful. The presence of a child in a home sweetens and refines. A child brought up in the fear of the Lord is a blessing.

Care and affection for dependent children removes the roughness from our natures, makes us tender and sympathetic, and has an influence to develop the nobler elements of our character.

After the birth of his first son, Enoch reached a higher experience; he was drawn into a closer relationship with God. He realized more fully his own obligations and responsibility as a son of God. And as he saw the child's love for its father, its simple trust in his protection; as he felt the deep, yearning tenderness of his own heart for that firstborn son, he learned a precious lesson of the wonderful love of God to men in the gift of His Son, and the confidence which the children of God may repose in their heavenly Father.

A Precious Trust: Children are committed to their parents as a precious trust, which God will one day require at their hands. We should give to their training more time, more care, and more prayer. They need more of the right kind of instruction.

Remember that your sons and daughters are younger members of God's family. He has committed them to your care, to train and educate for heaven. You must render an account to Him for the manner in which you discharge your sacred trust.

PLANNING THE SIZE OF YOUR FAMILY

A Grievous Wrong to Children: There are parents who, without consideration as to whether or not they can do justice to a large family, fill their houses with these helpless little beings, who are wholly dependent upon their parents for care and instruction. This is a grievous wrong, not only to the mother, but to her children and to society.

Has the mother sufficient strength to care for her children? And can the father give such advantages as will rightly mold and educate the child? How little is the destiny of the child considered! The gratification of passion is the only thought, and burdens are brought upon the wife and mother which undermine her vitality and paralyze her spiritual power. In broken health and with discouraged spirits she finds herself surrounded by a little flock whom she cannot care for as she should. Lacking the instruction they should have, they grow up to dishonor God and to communicate to others the evil of their own natures, and thus an army is raised up whom Satan manages as he pleases.

Other Factors: God would have parents act as rational beings and live in such a manner that each child may be properly educated, that the mother may have strength and time to employ her mental powers in disciplining her little ones for the society of the angels. She should have courage to act nobly her part and to do her work in the fear and love of God, that her children may prove a blessing to the family and to society.

The husband and father should consider all these things lest the wife and mother of his children be overtaxed and thus overwhelmed with despondency. He should see to it that the mother of his children is not placed in a position where she cannot possibly do justice to her numerous little ones, so that they have to come up without proper training.

Parents should not increase their families any faster than they know that their children can be well cared for and educated. A child in the mother's arms from year to year is great injustice to her. It lessens, and often destroys, social enjoyment and increases domestic wretchedness. It robs their children of that care, education, and happiness which parents should feel it their duty to bestow upon them.

Counsel to Parents of a Large Family: The question to be settled by you is, "Am I raising a family of children to strengthen the influence and swell the ranks of the powers of darkness, or

41

am I bringing up children for Christ?"

If you do not govern your children and mold their characters to meet the requirements of God, then the fewer children there are to suffer from your defective training the better it will be for you, their parents, and the better it will be for society. Unless children can be trained and disciplined from their babyhood by a wise and judicious mother who is conscientious and intelligent, and who rules her household in the fear of the Lord, molding and shaping their characters to meet the standard of righteousness, it is a sin to increase your family. God has given you reason, and He requires you to use it.

Economic Considerations: Parents should calmly consider what provision can be made for their children. They have no right to bring children into the world to be a burden to others. Have they a business that they can rely upon to sustain a family so that they need not become a burden to others? If they have not, they commit a crime in bringing children into the world to suffer for want of proper care, food, and clothing.

Those who are seriously deficient in business tact, and who are the least qualified to get along in the world, generally fill their houses with children; while men who have ability to acquire property generally have no more children than they can well provide for. Those who are not qualified to take care of themselves should not have children.

PARENTS' LEGACY TO CHILDREN

The Law of Heredity: The physical and mental condition of the parents is perpetuated in their offspring. This is a matter that is not duly considered. Wherever the habits of the parents are contrary to physical law, the injury done to themselves will be repeated in the future generations.

By physical, mental, and moral culture all may become co-workers with Christ. Very much depends upon the parents. It lies with them whether they shall bring into the world children who will prove a blessing or a curse.

The nobler the aims, the higher the mental and spiritual endowments, and the better developed the physical powers of the parents, the better will be the life equipment they give their children. In cultivating that which is best in themselves, parents are exerting an influence to mold society and to uplift future generations.

Many Parents Are Ignorant: Those who have charge of God's property in the souls and bodies of the children formed in His image should erect barriers against the sensual indulgence of this age which is ruining the physical and moral health of thousands. If the many crimes of this time were traced to their true cause, it would be seen that they are chargeable to the ignorance of fathers and mothers who are indifferent on this subject. Health and life itself is being sacrificed to this lamentable ignorance.

Parents, if you fail to give your children the education that God makes it your duty to give them, both by precept and example, you must answer to your God for the results. These results will not be confined merely to your children. They will reach through generations. Just as the one thistle permitted to grow in the field produces a harvest of its kind, the sins resulting from your neglect will work to ruin all who come within the sphere of their influence.

Reason for Double Understanding and Patience: Fathers and mothers may study their own character in their children. They may often read humiliating lessons as they see their own imperfections reproduced in their sons and daughters. While seeking to repress and correct in their children hereditary tendencies to evil, parents should call to their aid double patience, perseverance, and love.

When a child reveals the wrong traits which it has inherited from its parents, shall they storm over this reproduction of their own defects? No, no! Let parents keep a careful watch over themselves, guarding against all coarseness and roughness, lest these defects be seen once more in their children.

Manifest the meekness and gentleness of Christ in dealing with the wayward little ones. Always bear in mind that they have received their perversity as an inheritance from the father or mother. Then bear with the children who have inherited your own trait of character.

Parents must trust implicitly in the power of Christ to transform the tendencies to wrong which have been transmitted to their children.

Have patience, fathers and mothers. Often your past neglect will make your work hard. But God will give you strength if you will trust in Him. Deal wisely and tenderly with your children.

A SACRED CIRCLE

Sanctity of the Family Circle: There is a sacred circle around every family which should be preserved. No other one has any right in that sacred circle.

The husband and wife should be all to each other. The wife should have no secrets to keep from her husband and let others know, and the husband should have no secrets to keep from his wife to relate to others. The heart of his wife should be the grave for the faults of the husband, and the heart of the husband the grave for his wife's faults.

Never should either party indulge in a joke at the expense of the other's feelings. Never should either the husband or wife in sport or in any other manner complain of each other to others, for frequently indulging in this foolish and what may seem perfectly harmless joking will end in trial with each other and perhaps estrangement. There should be a sacred shield around every family.

The home circle should be regarded as a sacred place, a symbol of heaven, a mirror in which to reflect ourselves. Friends and acquaintances we may have, but in the homelife they are not to meddle. A strong sense of proprietorship should be felt, giving a sense of ease, restfulness, trust.

Patience, Forbearance, Forgiveness: Let those composing the family circle pray that God will sanctify their tongues, their ears, their eyes, and every member of their body. When brought into contact with evil, it is not necessary to be overcome of evil. Christ has made it possible for the character to be fragrant with good.

How many dishonor Christ and misrepresent His character in the home circle! How many do not manifest patience, forbearance, forgiveness, and true love! Many have their likes and dislikes and feel at liberty to manifest their own perverse disposition rather than to reveal the will, the works, the character, of Christ. The life of Jesus is full of kindness and love. Are we growing into His divine nature?

Parents should be careful not to allow the spirit of dissension to creep into the home; for this is one of Satan's agents to make his impression on the character. If parents will strive for unity in the home by inculcating the principles that governed the life of Christ, dissension will be driven out, and unity and love will abide there. Parents and children will partake of the gift of the Holy Spirit.

Let the husband and wife remember that they have burdens enough to carry without making their lives wretched by allowing differences to come in. Those who give place to little differences invite Satan into their home. The children catch the spirit of contention over mere trifles. Evil agencies do their part to make parents and children disloyal to God.

Although trials may arise in the married life, the husband and the wife are to keep their souls in the love of God. The father should look upon the mother of his children as one deserving of all kindness, tenderness, and sympathy.

The Secret of Family Unity: The cause of division and discord in families is separation from Christ. To come near to Christ is to come near to one another. The secret of true unity in the family is not diplomacy, not management, not a superhuman effort to overcome difficulties—though there will be much of this to do—but union with Christ.

Picture a large circle, from the edge of which are many lines all running to the center. The nearer these lines approach the center, the nearer they are to one another.

Thus it is in the Christian life. The closer we come to Christ, the nearer we shall be to one another.

Let Each Help the Other: The family firm is a sacred, social society, in which each member is to act a part, each helping the other. The work of the household is to move smoothly, like the different parts of well-regulated machinery.

Every member of the family should realize that a responsibility rests upon him individually to do his part in adding to the comfort, order, and regularity of the family. One should not work against another. All should unitedly engage in the good work of encouraging one another; they should exercise gentleness, forbearance, and patience; speak in low, calm tones, shunning confusion; and each doing his utmost to lighten the burdens of the mother.

Each member of the family should understand just the part he is expected to act in union with the others. All, from the child six years old and upward, should understand that it is required of them to bear their share of life's burdens.

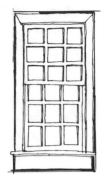

YOUR CHILD'S FIRST SCHOOL

The Family Circle a School: In His wisdom the Lord has decreed that the family shall be the greatest of all educational agencies. It is in the home that the education of the child is to begin. Here is his first school. Here, with his parents as instructors, he is to learn the lessons that are to guide him throughout life—lessons of respect, obedience, reverence, self-control.

The educational influences of the home are a decided power for good or for evil. They are in many respects silent and gradual, but if exerted on the right side, they become a far-reaching power for truth and righteousness. If the child is not instructed aright here, Satan will educate him through agencies of his choosing. How important, then, is the school in the home!

Look upon the family circle as a training school, where you are preparing your children for the performance of their duties at home, in society, and in the church.

Home Education First in Importance: It is a sad fact, almost universally admitted and deplored, that the home education and training of the youth of today have been neglected.

There is no more important field of effort than that committed to the founders and guardians of the home. No work entrusted to human beings involves greater or more far-reaching results than does the work of fathers and mothers.

It is by the youth and children of today that the future of society is to be determined, and what these youth and children shall be depends upon the home. To the lack of right home training may be traced the larger share of the disease and misery and crime that curse humanity. If the homelife were pure and true, if the children who went forth from its care were prepared to meet life's responsibilities and dangers, what a change would be seen in the world!

All Else to Be Secondary: Every child brought into the world is the property of Jesus Christ, and should be educated by precept and example to love and obey God; but by far the largest number of parents have neglected their God-given work, by failing to educate and train their children, from the first dawning of reason, to know and love Christ. By painstaking effort parents are to watch the opening, receptive mind and make everything in the homelife secondary to the positive duty enjoined upon them by God—to train their children in the nurture and admonition of the Lord.

Parents should not permit business cares, worldly customs and maxims, and fashion to have a controlling power over them, so that they neglect their children in babyhood and fail to give their children proper instruction as they increase in years.

One great reason why there is so much evil in the world today is that parents occupy their minds with other things than that which is all-important—how to adapt themselves to the work of patiently and kindly teaching their children the way of the Lord. If the curtain could be drawn aside, we should see that many, many children who have gone astray have been lost to good influences through this neglect. Parents, can you afford to have it so in your experience? You should have no work so important that it will prevent you from giving to your children all the time that is necessary to make them understand what it means to obey and trust the Lord fully.

And what will you reap as a reward of your effort? You will find your children right by your side, willing to take hold and cooperate with you in the lines that you suggest. You will find your work made easy.

The mother must ever stand preeminent in this work of training the children; while grave and important duties rest upon the father, the mother, by almost constant association with her children, especially during their tender years, must always be their special instructor and companion. She should take great care to cultivate neatness and order in her children, to direct them in forming correct habits and tastes; she should train them to be industrious, self-reliant, and helpful to others; to live and act and labor as though always in the sight of God.

Parents should be much at home. By precept and example they should teach their children the love and the fear of God; teach them to be intelligent, social, affectionate; to cultivate habits of industry, economy, and self-denial. By giving their children love, sympathy, and encouragement at home, parents may provide for them a safe and welcome retreat from many of the world's temptations.

God's Injunctions to Be Paramount: We have Bible rules

for the guidance of all, both parents and children, a high and holy standard from which there can be no swerving. God's injunctions must be paramount. Let the father and mother of the family spread out God's Word before Him, the searcher of hearts, and ask in sincerity, "What hath God said?"

Responsibilities Only Parents Can Carry: Parents, you carry responsibilities that no one can bear for you. As long as you live, you are accountable to God to keep His way. Parents who make the Word of God their guide, and who realize how much their children depend upon them for the characters they form, will set an example that it will be safe for their children to follow.

Fathers and mothers are responsible for the health, the constitution, the development of the character of their children. No one else should be left to see to this work. In becoming the parents of children, it devolves upon you to cooperate with the Lord in educating them in sound principles.

How sad it is that many parents have cast off their God-given responsibility to their children, and are willing that strangers should bear it for them! They are willing that others should labor for their children and relieve them of all burden in the matter.

Many who are now bemoaning the waywardness of their children have only themselves to blame. Let these look to their Bibles and see what God enjoins upon them as parents and guardians. Let them take up their long-neglected duties. They need to humble themselves and to repent before God for their neglect to follow His directions in the training of their children. They need to change their own course of action and to follow the Bible strictly and carefully as their guide and counselor.

FAMILY COMPANIONSHIP

Become Acquainted With Your Children: Some parents do not understand their children and are not really acquainted with them. There is often a great distance between parents and children. If the parents would enter more fully into the feelings of their children and draw out what is in their hearts, it would have a beneficial influence upon them.

Parents should study the best and most successful manner of winning the love and confidence of their children, that they may lead them in the right path. They should reflect the sunshine of love upon the household.

Encouragement and Commendation: Young children love companionship and can seldom enjoy themselves alone. They yearn for sympathy and tenderness. That which they enjoy they think will please mother also, and it is natural for them to go to her with their little joys and sorrows. The mother should not wound their sensitive hearts by treating with indifference matters that, though trifling to her, are of great importance to them. Her sympathy and approval are precious. An approving glance, a word of encouragement or commendation, will be like sunshine in their hearts, often making the whole day happy.

Parents to Be Child's Confidants: Parents should encourage their children to confide in *them* and unburden to them their heart griefs, their little daily annoyances and trials.

Kindly instruct them and bind them to your hearts. It is a critical time for children. Influences will be thrown around them to wean them from you which you must counteract. Teach them to make you their confidant. Let them whisper in your ear their trials and joys.

Children would be saved from many evils if they would be more familiar with their parents. Parents should encourage in their children a disposition to be open and frank with them, to come to them with their difficulties and, when they are perplexed as to what course is right, to lay the matter just as they view it before the parents and ask their advice.

Who are so well calculated to see and point out their dangers as godly parents? Who can understand the peculiar temperaments of their own children as well as they? The mother who has watched every turn of the mind from infancy, and is thus acquainted with the natural disposition, is best prepared to counsel her children. Who can tell as well what traits of char-

53

acter to check and restrain as the mother, aided by the father?

Never, Never Neglect Your Children: "No time," says the father; "I have no time to give to the training of my children, no time for social and domestic enjoyments." Then you should not have taken upon yourself the responsibility of a family. By withholding from them the time which is justly theirs, you rob them of the education which they should have at your hands. If you have children, you have a work to do, in union with the mother, in the formation of their characters.

It is the cry of many mothers: "I have no time to be with my children." Then for Christ's sake spend less time on your dress. Neglect if you will to adorn your apparel. Neglect to receive and make calls. Neglect to cook an endless variety of dishes. But never, never neglect your children. What is the chaff to the wheat? Let nothing interpose between you and the best interests of your children.

Burdened with many cares, mothers sometimes feel that they cannot take time patiently to instruct their little ones and give them love and sympathy. But they should remember that if the children do not find in their parents and in their home that which will satisfy their desire for sympathy and companionship, they will look to other sources, where both mind and character may be endangered.

With Your Children in Work and Play: Give some of your leisure hours to your children; associate with them in their work and in their sports, and win their confidence. Cultivate their friendship.

Let parents devote the evenings to their families. Lay off care and perplexity with the labors of the day.

Narrowing the Generation Gap: There is danger of both parents and teachers commanding and dictating too much, while they fail to come sufficiently into social relation with their children or scholars. They often hold themselves too much reserved and exercise their authority in a cold, unsympathizing manner which cannot win the hearts of their children and pupils. If they would gather the children close to them and show that they love them, and would manifest an interest in all their efforts and even in their sports, sometimes even being a child among children, they would make the children very happy and would gain their love and win their confidence. And the children would sooner respect and love the authority of their parents and teachers.

No barrier of coldness and reserve should be allowed to arise between parents and children. Let parents become acquainted with their children, seeking to understand their tastes and dispositions, entering into their feelings, and drawing out what is in their hearts.

Parents, let your children see that you love them and will do all in your power to make them happy. If you do so, your necessary restrictions will have far greater weight in their young minds. Rule your children with tenderness and compassion, remembering that "their angels do always behold the face of my Father which is in heaven." If you desire the angels to do for your children the work given them of God, cooperate with them by doing your part.

Brought up under the wise and loving guidance of a true home, children will have no desire to wander away in search of pleasure and companionship. Evil will not attract them. The spirit that prevails in the home will mold their characters; they will form habits and principles that will be a strong defense against temptation when they shall leave the home shelter and take their place in the world.

SECURITY

THROUGH LOVE

The Power of Love: Love's agencies have wonderful power, for they are divine. The soft answer that "turneth away wrath," the love that "suffereth long, and is kind," the charity that "covereth a multitude of sins"—would we learn the lesson, with what power for healing would our lives be gifted! How life would be transformed and the earth become a very likeness and foretaste of heaven!

These precious lessons may be so simply taught as to be understood even by little children. The heart of the child is tender and easily impressed; and when we who are older become "as little children," when we learn the simplicity and gentleness and tender love of the Saviour, we shall not find it difficult to touch the hearts of the little ones and teach them love's ministry of healing.

From a worldly point of view, money is power; but from the Christian standpoint, love is power. Intellectual and spiritual strength are involved in this principle. Pure love has special efficacy to do good, and can do nothing but good. It prevents discord and misery and brings the truest happiness. Wealth is often an influence to corrupt and destroy; force is strong to do hurt; but truth and goodness are the properties of pure love.

Remember Your Own Childhood: Do not treat your children only with sternness, forgetting your own childhood and forgetting that they are but children. Do not expect them to be perfect or try to make them men and women in their acts at once. By so doing, you will close the door of access which you might otherwise have to them and will drive them to open a door for injurious influences, for others to poison their young minds before you awake to their danger.

Parents should not forget their childhood years, how much they yearned for sympathy and love, and how unhappy they felt when censured and fretfully chided. They should be young again in their feelings, and bring their minds down to understand the wants of their children.

Parents, give your children love: love in babyhood, love in childhood, love in youth. Do not give them frowns, but ever keep a sunshiny countenance.

Keep Children in a Sunny Atmosphere: The little ones must be carefully soothed when in trouble. Children between babyhood and manhood and womanhood do not generally receive the attention that they should have. Mothers are needed who will so guide their children that they will regard themselves as a part of the family. Let the mother talk with her children regarding their hopes and their perplexities. Let parents remember that their children are to be cared for in preference to strangers. They are to be kept in a sunny atmosphere, under the mother's guidance.

Satisfy Reasonable Wants: You should ever impress upon your children the fact that you love them; that you are laboring for their interest; that their happiness is dear to you; and that

57

you design to do only that which is for their good. You should gratify their little wants whenever you can reasonably do so.

Never act from impulse in governing children. Let authority and affection be blended. Cherish and cultivate all that is good and lovely, and lead them to desire the higher good by revealing Christ to them. While you deny them those things that would be an injury to them, let them see that you love them and want to make them happy. The more unlovely they are, the greater pains you should take to reveal your love for them. When the child has confidence that you want to make him happy, love will break every barrier down.

Express Your Love: In many families there is a great lack in expressing affection one for another. While there is no need of sentimentalism, there is need of expressing love and tenderness in a chaste, pure, dignified way. Many absolutely cultivate hardness of heart and in word and action reveal the satanic side of the character. Tender affection should ever be cherished between husband and wife, parents and children, brothers and sisters. Every hasty word should be checked, and there should not be even the appearance of the lack of love one for another. It is the duty of everyone in the family to be pleasant, to speak kindly.

Cultivate tenderness, affection, and love that have expression in little courtesies, in speech, in thoughtful attentions.

Mirror the Love of Jesus: When the mother has gained the confidence of her children and taught them to love and obey her, she has given them the first lesson in the Christian life. They must love and trust and obey their Saviour as they love and trust and obey their parents. The love which in faithful care and right training the parent manifests for the child faintly mirrors the love of Jesus for His faithful people.

GARDEN OF THE HEART

Parents as Gardeners: The Lord has entrusted to parents a solemn, sacred work. They are to cultivate carefully the soil of the heart. Thus they may be laborers together with God. He expects them to guard and tend carefully the garden of their children's hearts. They are to sow the good seed, weeding out every unsightly weed. Every defect in character, every fault in disposition, needs to be cut away; for if allowed to remain, these will mar the beauty of the character.

Tending the Garden: The prevailing influence in the world is to suffer the youth to follow the natural turn of their own minds. And if very wild in youth, parents say they will come right after a while and, when sixteen or eighteen years of age, will reason for themselves and leave off their wrong habits and become at last useful men and women. What a mistake! For years they permit an enemy to sow the garden of the heart; they suffer wrong principles to grow, and in many cases all the labor afterward bestowed on that soil will avail nothing.

Some parents have suffered their children to form wrong habits, the marks of which may be seen all through life. Upon the parents lies this sin. These children may profess to be Christians; yet without a special work of grace upon the heart and a thorough reform in life, their past habits will be seen in all their experience, and they will exhibit just the character which their parents allowed them to form.

The young should not be suffered to learn good and evil indiscriminately, with the idea that at some future time the good will predominate and the evil lose its influence. The evil will increase faster than the good. It is possible that after many years the evil they have learned may be eradicated; but who will venture this? Time is short. It is easier and much safer to sow clean, good seed in the hearts of your children than to pluck up the weeds afterward. Impressions made upon the minds of the young are hard to efface. How important, then, that these impressions be of the right sort, that the elastic faculties of youth be bent in the right direction.

Seed Sowing and Weeding: In the earliest years of the child's life the soil of the heart should be carefully prepared for the showers of God's grace. Then the seeds of truth are to be carefully sown and diligently tended. And God, who rewards every effort made in His name, will put life into the seed sown; and there will appear first the blade, then the ear, then the full corn in the ear.

If a field is left uncultivated, a crop of noxious weeds is sure to appear which will be very difficult to exterminate. Then the soil must be worked and the weeds subdued before the precious plants can grow. Before these valuable plants can grow, the seed must first be carefully sown. If mothers neglect the sowing of the precious seed and then expect a harvest of precious grain, they will be disappointed; for they will reap briars and thorns. Satan is ever watching, prepared to sow seeds which will spring up and bear a plentiful harvest after his own satanic character.

 **PROMISES OF DIVINE GUIDANCE**

Jesus, the Mother's Divine Friend: Your compassionate Redeemer is watching you with love and sympathy, ready to hear your prayers and to render you the assistance which you need. He knows the burdens of every mother's heart and is her best friend in every emergency. His everlasting arms support the God-fearing, faithful mother.

When upon earth, He had a mother that struggled with poverty, having many anxious cares and perplexities, and He sympathizes with every Christian mother in her cares and anxieties. That Saviour who took a long journey for the purpose of relieving the anxious heart of a woman whose daughter was possessed by an evil spirit will hear the mother's prayers and will bless her children.

He who gave back to the widow her only son as he was carried to the burial is touched today by the woe of the bereaved mother. He who wept tears of sympathy at the grave of Lazarus and gave back to Martha and Mary their buried brother; who pardoned Mary Magdalene; who remembered His mother when He was hanging in agony upon the cross; who appeared to the weeping women and made them His messengers to spread the first glad tidings of a risen Saviour—He is woman's best friend today and is ready to aid her in all the relations of life.

No work can equal that of the Christian mother. She takes up her work with a sense of what it is to bring up her children in the nurture and admonition of the Lord. How often will she feel her burden's weight heavier than she can bear; and then how precious the privilege of taking it all to her sympathizing Saviour in prayer! She may lay her burden at His feet and find in His presence a strength that will sustain her and give her cheerfulness, hope, courage, and wisdom in the most trying hours. How sweet to the careworn mother is the consciousness of such a friend in all her difficulties! If mothers would go to Christ more frequently and trust Him more fully, their burdens would be easier, and they would find rest to their souls.

God Hears Your Prayers: Parents may understand that as they follow God's directions in the training of their children, they will receive help from on high. They receive much benefit; for as they teach, they learn. Their children will achieve victories through the knowledge that they have acquired in keeping the way of the Lord. They are enabled to overcome natural and hereditary tendencies to evil.

Parents, are you working with unflagging energy in behalf of your children? The God of heaven marks your solicitude, your earnest work, your constant watchfulness. He hears your prayers. With patience and tenderness train your children for the Lord. All heaven is interested in your work. God will unite with you, crowning your efforts with success.

As you try to make plain the truths of salvation, and point the children to Christ as a personal Saviour, angels will be by your side. The Lord will give to fathers and mothers grace to interest their little ones in the precious story of the Babe of Bethlehem, who is indeed the hope of the world.

Ask and Receive: In their important work parents must ask and receive divine aid. Even if the character, habits, and practices of parents have been cast in an inferior mold, if the lessons given them in childhood and youth have led to an unhappy development of character, they need not despair. The converting power of God can transform inherited and cultivated tendencies, for the religion of Jesus is uplifting. "Born again" means a transformation, a new birth in Christ Jesus.

Let us instruct our children in the teachings of the Word. If you will call, the Lord will answer you. He will say, Here I am; what would you have Me do for you? Heaven is linked with earth that every soul may be enabled to fulfill his mission. The Lord loves these children. He wants them brought up with an understanding of their high calling.

The Holy Spirit Will Guide: Christ has made every provision that every parent who will be controlled by the Holy Spirit will be given strength and grace to be a teacher in the home. This education and discipline in the home will have a molding and fashioning influence.

Uniting Divine Power and Human Effort: Without human effort divine effort is in vain. God will work with power when in trustful dependence upon Him parents will awake to the sacred responsibility resting upon them and seek to train their children aright. He will cooperate with those parents who carefully and prayerfully educate their children, working out their own and their children's salvation. He will work in them to will and to do of His own good pleasure.

Human effort alone will not result in helping your children to perfect a character for heaven; but with divine help a grand and holy work may be accomplished.

Work in Faith: Patiently, lovingly, as faithful stewards of the manifold grace of Christ, parents are to do their appointed work. It is expected of them that they will be found faithful. Everything is to be done in faith. Constantly they must pray that God will impart His grace to their children. Never must they become weary, impatient, or fretful in their work. They must cling closely to their children and to God. If parents work in patience and love, earnestly endeavoring to help their children to reach the highest standard of purity and modesty, they will succeed.

FATHER'S RESPONSIBILITIES

Definition of Husband: The work of making home happy does not rest upon the mother alone. Fathers have an important part to act. The husband is the house-band of the home treasures, binding by his strong, earnest, devoted affection the members of the household, mother and children, together in the strongest bonds of union.

Head of the Family: The husband and father is the head of the household. The wife looks to him for love and sympathy and for aid in the training of the children; and this is right. The children are his as well as hers, and he is equally interested in their welfare. The children look to the father for support and guidance; he needs to have a right conception of life and of the influences and associations that should surround his family; above all, he should be controlled by the love and fear of God and by the teaching of His Word, that he may guide the feet of his children in the right way.

The father should do his part toward making home happy. Whatever his cares and business perplexities, they should not be permitted to overshadow his family; he should enter his home with smiles and pleasant words.

Maturity of Experience Called For: A father must not be as a child, moved merely by impulse. He is bound to his family by sacred, holy ties.

What his influence will be in the home will be determined by his knowledge of the only true God and Jesus Christ whom He has sent. "When I was a child," Paul says, "I spake as a child, I understood as a child, I thought as a child: but when I became a man, I put away childish things."

The father is to stand at the head of his family, not as an overgrown, undisciplined boy, but as a man with manly character and with his passions controlled. He is to obtain an education in correct morals. His conduct in his homelife is to be directed and restrained by the pure principles of the Word of God. Then he will grow up to the full stature of a man in Christ Jesus.

Submit the Will to God: To the man who is a husband and a father, I would say, Be sure that a pure, holy atmosphere surrounds your soul. You are to learn daily of Christ. Never, never are you to show a tyrannical spirit in the home. The man who does this is working in partnership with satanic agencies. Bring your will into submission to the will of God. Do all in your power to make the life of your wife pleasant and happy. Take the Word of God as the man of your counsel. In the home live out the teachings of the Word. Then you will live them out in the church and will take them with you to your place of business. The principles of heaven will ennoble all your transactions. Angels of God will cooperate with you, helping you to reveal Christ to the world.

Exercise Authority With Humility: It is no evidence of manliness in the husband for him to dwell constantly upon his position as head of the family. It does not increase respect for him to hear him quoting Scripture to sustain his claims to authority. It will not make him more manly to require his wife, the mother of his children, to act upon his plans as if they were infallible.

The Lord has constituted the husband the head of the wife to be her protector; he is the house-band of the family, binding the members together, even as Christ is the head of the church and the Saviour of the mystical body. Let every husband who claims to love God carefully study the requirements of God in his position. Christ's authority is exercised in wisdom, in all kindness and gentleness; so let the husband exercise his power and imitate the great Head of the church.

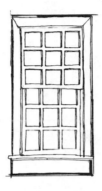

SHARING
THE
BURDENS

A Nontransferable Duty: The father's duty to his children cannot be transferred to the mother. If she performs her own duty, she has burden enough to bear. Only by working in unison can the father and mother accomplish the work which God has committed to their hands.

The father should not excuse himself from his part in the work of educating his children for life and immortality. He must share in the responsibility. There is obligation for both father and mother. There must be love and respect manifested by the parents for one another, if they would see these qualities developed in their children.

The father should encourage and sustain the mother in her work of care by his cheerful looks and kind words.

Father to Lighten Mother's Load: Whatever may be his calling and its perplexities, let the father take into his home the same smiling countenance and pleasant tones with which he has all day greeted visitors and strangers. Let the wife feel that she can lean upon the large affections of her husband—that his arms will strengthen and uphold her through all her toils and cares, that his influence will sustain hers—and her burden will lose half its weight.

Domestic duties are sacred and important; yet they are often attended by a weary monotony. The countless cares and perplexities become irritating without the variety of change and cheerful relaxation which the husband and father frequently has in his power to grant her if he chose—or rather if he thought it necessary or desirable to do so. The life of a mother in the humbler walks of life is one of unceasing self-sacrifice, made harder if the husband fails to appreciate the difficulties of her position and to give her his support.

Show Consideration for a Feeble Wife: The husband should manifest great interest in his family. Especially should he be very tender of the feelings of a feeble wife. He can shut the door against much disease.

Kind, cheerful, and encouraging words will prove more effective than the most healing medicines. These will bring courage to the heart of the desponding and discouraged, and the happiness and sunshine brought into the family by kind acts and encouraging words will repay the effort tenfold.

The husband should remember that much of the burden of training his children rests upon the mother, that she has much to do with molding their minds. This should call into exercise his tenderest feelings, and with care should he lighten her burdens.

He should encourage her to lean upon his large affections and direct her mind to heaven, where there is strength and peace and a final rest for the weary. He should not come to his home with a clouded brow, but should with his presence bring sunlight into the family and should encourage his wife to look up and believe in God. Unitedly they can claim the promises of God and bring His rich blessing into the family.

"Lead on Softly": Many a husband and father might learn a helpful lesson from the carefulness of the faithful shepherd. Jacob, when urged to undertake a rapid and difficult journey, made answer:

"The children are tender, and the flocks and herds with young are with me: and if men should overdrive them one day, all the flock will die."

"I will lead on softly, according as the cattle that goeth before me and the children be able to endure."

In life's toilsome way let the husband and father "lead on softly," as the companion of his journey is able to endure. Amidst the world's eager rush for wealth and power, let him learn to stay his steps, to comfort and support the one who is called to walk by his side.

Let the husband aid his wife by his sympathy and unfailing affection. If he wishes to keep her fresh and gladsome, so that she will be as sunshine in the home, let him help her bear her burdens. His kindness and loving courtesy will be to her a precious encouragement, and the happiness he imparts will bring joy and peace to his own heart.

69

A COMPANION WITH HIS CHILDREN

Spend Time With Children: The average father wastes many golden opportunities to attract and bind his children to him. Upon returning home from his business, he should find it a pleasant change to spend some time with his children.

Fathers should unbend from their false dignity, deny themselves some slight self-gratification in time and leisure, in order to mingle with the children, sympathizing with them in their little troubles, binding them to their hearts by the strong bonds of love, and establishing such an influence over their expanding minds that their counsel will be regarded as sacred.

Take Special Interest in the Boys: The father of boys should come into close contact with his sons, giving them the benefit of his larger experience and talking with them in such simplicity and tenderness that he binds them to his heart. He should let them see that he has their best interest, their happiness, in view all the time.

Train Children for Usefulness: The father, as the head of his own household, should understand how to train his children for usefulness and duty. This is his special work, above every other. During the first few years of a child's life the molding of the disposition is committed principally to the mother; but she should ever feel that in her work she has the cooperation of the father. If he is engaged in business which almost wholly closes the door of usefulness to his family, he should seek other employment which will not prevent him from devoting some time to his children. If he neglects them, he is unfaithful to the trust committed to him of God.

Fathers, spend as much time as possible with your children. Seek to become acquainted with their various dispositions, that you may know how to train them in harmony with the Word of God. Never should a word of discouragement pass your lips. Do not bring darkness into the home. Be pleasant, kind, and affectionate toward your children, but not foolishly indulgent. Let them bear their little disappointments, as everyone must. Do not encourage them to come to you with their petty complaints of one another. Teach them to bear with one another and to seek to maintain each other's confidence and respect.

With Them in Work and Sports: Fathers, combine affection with authority, kindness and sympathy with firm restraint. Give some of your leisure hours to your children; become acquainted with them; associate with them in their work and in their sports, and win their confidence. Cultivate friendship with them, especially with your sons. In this way you will be a strong influence for good.

71

TOLERANT, COURTEOUS HUSBANDS

Asking Too Much: In most families there are children of various ages, some of whom need not only the attention and wise discipline of the mother but also the sterner, yet affectionate, influence of the father. Few fathers consider this matter in its due importance. They fall into neglect of their own duty and thus heap grievous burdens upon the mother, at the same time feeling at liberty to criticize and condemn her actions according to their judgment.

Under this heavy sense of responsibility and censure, the poor wife and mother often feels guilty and remorseful for that which she has done innocently or ignorantly, and frequently when she has done the very best thing possible under the circumstances. Yet when her wearisome efforts should be appreciated and approved and her heart made glad, she is obliged to walk under a cloud of sorrow and condemnation because her husband, while ignoring his own duty, expects her to fulfill both her own and his to his satisfaction, regardless of preventing circumstances.

Many husbands do not sufficiently understand and appreciate the cares and perplexities which their wives endure, generally confined all day to an unceasing round of household duties. They frequently come to their homes with clouded brows, bringing no sunshine to the family circle. If the meals are not on time, the tired wife, who is frequently housekeeper, nurse, cook, and housemaid, all in one, is greeted with faultfinding.

The exacting husband may condescend to take the worrying child from the weary arms of its mother that her arrangements for the family meal may be hastened; but if the child is restless and frets in the arms of its father, he will seldom feel it his duty to act the nurse and seek to quiet and soothe it.

He does not pause to consider how many hours the mother had endured the little one's fretfulness, but calls out impatiently, "Here, Mother, take *your* child." Is it not *his* child as well as hers? Is he not under a natural obligation to patiently bear his part of the burden of rearing his children?

Fretful Husbands: Husbands, give your wives a chance for their spiritual life. By many the disposition to fret is encouraged until they become like grown-up children. They do not leave this portion of their child life behind them. They cherish these feelings until they cramp and dwarf the whole life by their querulous complaints—and not only their own lives but the lives of others also.

The husband and father who is morose, selfish, and overbearing is not only unhappy himself, but he casts gloom upon all the inmates of his home. He will reap the result in seeing his wife dispirited and sickly and his children marred with his own unlovely temper.

Counsel to an Intolerant Husband: You expect too much of your wife and children. You censure too much. If you would encourage a cheerful, happy temper yourself and speak kindly and tenderly to them, you would bring sunlight into your dwelling instead of clouds, sorrow, and unhappiness.

You think too much of your opinion; you have taken extreme positions, and have not been willing that your wife's judgment should have the weight it should in your family. You have not encouraged respect for your wife yourself nor educated your children to respect her judgment. You have not made her your equal, but have rather taken the reins of government and control into your own hands and held them with a firm grasp. You have not an affectionate, sympathetic disposition. These traits of character you need to cultivate if you want to be an overcomer and if you want the blessing of God in your family.

To One Who Disregards Christian Courtesy: You have looked upon it as a weakness to be kind, tender, and sympathetic and have thought it beneath your dignity to speak tenderly, gently, and lovingly to your wife. Here you mistake in what true manliness and dignity consist. The disposition to leave deeds of kindness undone is a manifest weakness and defect in your character. That which you would look upon as weakness God regards as true Christian courtesy that should be exercised by every Christian; for this was the spirit which Christ manifested.

Husbands Should Merit Love and Affection: If the husband is tyrannical, exacting, critical of the actions of his wife, he cannot hold her respect and affection, and the marriage relation will become odious to her. She will not love her husband, because he does not try to make himself lovable. Husbands should be careful, attentive, constant, faithful, and compassionate. They should manifest love and sympathy. When the husband has the nobility of character, purity of heart, elevation of mind, that every true Christian must possess, it will be made manifest in the marriage relation.

The Husband's Equal: Woman should fill the position which God originally designed for her, as her husband's equal. The world needs mothers who are mothers not merely in name but in every sense of the word. We may safely say that the distinctive duties of woman are more sacred, more holy, than those of man. Let woman realize the sacredness of her work and in the strength and fear of God take up her life mission. Let her educate her children for usefulness in this world and for a home in the better world.

The mother is the queen of the home, and the children are her subjects. She is to rule her household wisely, in the dignity of her motherhood. Her influence in the home is to be paramount; her word, law. If she is a Christian, under God's control, she will command the respect of her children.

The children are to be taught to regard their mother, not as a slave whose work it is to wait on them, but as a queen who is to guide and direct them, teaching them line upon line, precept upon precept.

A Graphic Comparison of Values: The mother seldom appreciates her own work and frequently sets so low an estimate upon her labor that she regards it as domestic drudgery. She goes through the same round day after day, week after week, with no special marked results. She cannot tell at the close of the day the many little things she has accomplished. Placed beside her husband's achievement, she feels that she has done nothing worth mentioning.

The father frequently comes in with a self-satisfied air and proudly recounts what he has accomplished through the day. His remarks show that now he must be waited upon by the mother, for she has not done much except take care of the children, cook the meals, and keep the house in order. She has not acted the merchant, bought nor sold; she has not acted the farmer, in tilling the soil; she has not acted the mechanic—therefore she has done nothing to make her weary. He criticizes and censures and dictates as though he was the lord of creation. And this is all the more trying to the wife and mother, because she has become very weary at her post of duty during the day, and yet she cannot see what she has done and is really disheartened.

Could the veil be withdrawn and father and mother see as God sees the work of the day, and see how His infinite eye compares the work of the one with that of the other, they would be astonished at the heavenly revelation. The father would view his labors in a more modest light, while the mother would have new courage and energy to pursue her labor with wisdom, perseverance, and patience. Now she knows its value. While the father has been dealing with the things which must perish and pass away, the mother has been dealing with developing minds and character, working not only for time but for eternity.

God Appointed Work: The mother who cheerfully takes up the duties lying directly in her path will feel that life is to her precious, because God has given her a work to perform. In this work she need not necessarily dwarf her mind nor allow her intellect to become enfeebled.

The mother's work is given her of God, to bring up her children in the nurture and admonition of the Lord. The love and fear of God should ever be kept before their tender minds.

When corrected, they should be taught to feel that they are admonished of God, that He is displeased with deception, untruthfulness, and wrongdoing. Thus the minds of little ones may be so connected with God that all they do and say will be in reference to His glory; and in afteryears they will not be like the reed in the wind, continually wavering between inclination and duty.

Amid all the activities of life the mother's most sacred duty is to her children. But how often is this duty put aside that some selfish gratification may be followed! Parents are entrusted with the present and eternal interests of their children. They are to hold the reins of government and guide their households to the honor of God. God's law should be their standard, and love should rule in all things.

The mother is God's agent to Christianize her family. She is to exemplify Biblical religion, showing how its influence is to control us in its everyday duties and pleasures, teaching her children that by grace alone can they be saved, through faith, which is the gift of God. This constant teaching as to what Christ is to us and to them, His love, His goodness, His mercy, revealed in the great plan of redemption, will make a hallowed, sacred impress on the heart.

A Life Mission: Let woman realize the sacredness of her work and, in the strength and fear of God, take up her life mission. Let her educate her children for usefulness in this world and for a fitness for the better world. We address Christian mothers. We entreat that you feel your responsibility as mothers and that you live not to please yourselves, but to glorify God. Christ pleased not Himself, but took upon Him the form of a servant.

The world teems with corrupting influences. Fashion and custom exert a strong power over the young. If the mother fails in her duty to instruct, guide, and restrain, her children will naturally accept the evil and turn from the good. Let every mother go often to her Saviour with the prayer, "Teach us, how shall we order the child, and what shall we do unto him?" Let her heed the instruction which God has given in His Word, and wisdom will be given her as she shall have need.

Sculpturing a Divine Likeness: There is a God above, and the light and glory from His throne rests upon the faithful mother as she tries to educate her children to resist the influence of evil. No other work can equal hers in importance. She has not, like the artist, to paint a form of beauty upon canvas; nor, like the sculptor, to chisel it from marble. She has not, like the author, to embody a noble thought in words of power; nor, like the musician, to express a beautiful sentiment in melody. It is hers, with the help of God, to develop in a human soul the likeness of the divine.

The mother who appreciates this will regard her opportunities as priceless. Earnestly will she seek, in her own character and by her methods of training, to present before her children the highest ideal. Earnestly, patiently, courageously, she will endeavor to improve her own abilities, that she may use aright the highest powers of the mind in the training of her children. Earnestly will she inquire at every step, "What hath God spoken?" Diligently she will study His Word. She will keep her eyes fixed upon Christ, that her own daily experience, in the lowly round of care and duty, may be a true reflection of the one true Life.

Let every mother feel that her moments are priceless; her work will be tested in the solemn day of accounts. Then it will be found that many of the failures and crimes of men and women have resulted from the ignorance and neglect of those whose duty it was to guide their childish feet in the right way. Then it will be found that many who have blessed the world with the light of genius and truth and holiness owe the principles that were the mainspring of their influence and success to a praying, Christian mother.

THE MOTHER'S INFLUENCE

Mother's Eternal Influence: The sphere of the mother may be humble; but her influence, united with the father's, is as abiding as eternity. Next to God, the mother's power for good is the strongest known on earth.

Little does the mother realize that her influence in the judicious training of her children reaches with such power through the vicissitudes of this life, stretching forward into the future, immortal life. To fashion a character after the heavenly Model requires much faithful, earnest, persevering labor; but it will pay, for God is a rewarder of all well-directed labor in securing the salvation of souls.

Like Mother, Like Children: The tenderest earthly tie is that between the mother and her child. The child is more readily impressed by the life and example of the mother than by that of the father, for a stronger and more tender bond of union unites them.

The thoughts and feelings of the mother will have a powerful influence upon the legacy she gives her child. If she allows her mind to dwell upon her own feelings, if she indulges in selfishness, if she is peevish and exacting, the disposition of her child will testify to the fact. Thus many have received as a birthright almost unconquerable tendencies to evil. The enemy of souls understands this matter much better than do many parents. He will bring his temptations to bear upon the mother, knowing that if she does not resist him, he can through her affect her child. The mother's only hope is in God. She may flee to Him for strength and grace; and she will not seek in vain.

The Patient Mother: Many times in the day is the cry of, "Mother, mother," heard, first from one little troubled voice and then another. In answer to the cry, mother must turn here and there to attend to their demands. One is in trouble and needs the wise head of the mother to free him from his perplexity. Another is so pleased with some of his devices he must have his mother see them, thinking she will be as pleased as he is. A word of approval will bring sunshine to the heart for hours. Many precious beams of light and gladness can the mother shed here and there among her precious little ones. How closely can she bind these dear ones to her heart, that her presence will be to them the sunniest place in the world.

But frequently the patience of the mother is taxed with these numerous little trials that seem scarcely worth attention. Mischievous hands and restless feet create a great amount of labor and perplexity for the mother. She has to hold fast the reins of self-control, or impatient words will slip from her tongue. She almost forgets herself time and again, but a silent prayer to her pitying Redeemer calms her nerves, and she is enabled to hold the reins of self-control with quiet dignity. She speaks with calm voice, but it has cost her an effort to restrain harsh words and subdue angry feelings which, if expressed, would have destroyed her influence, which it would have taken time to regain.

The World's Debt to Mothers: The day of God will reveal how much the world owes to godly mothers for men who have been unflinching advocates of truth and reform—men who have been bold to do and dare, who have stood unshaken amid trials and temptations; men who chose the high and holy interests of truth and the glory of God before worldly honor or life itself.

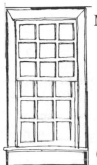 **MISCONCEPTION**

OF THE MOTHER'S WORK

Rarely Appreciated: The mother's work often seems to her an unimportant service. It is a work that is rarely appreciated. Others know little of her many cares and burdens.

Her days are occupied with a round of little duties, all calling for patient effort, for self-control, for tact, wisdom, and self-sacrificing love; yet she cannot boast of what she has done as any great achievement. She has only kept things in the home running smoothly. Often weary and perplexed, she has tried to speak kindly to the children, to keep them busy and happy, and to

81

guide their little feet in the right path. She feels that she has accomplished nothing.

But it is not so. Heavenly angels watch the careworn mother, noting the burdens she carries day by day. Her name may not have been heard in the world, but it is written in the Lamb's book of life.

Family Care Comes First: If you ignore your duty as a wife and mother and hold out your hands for the Lord to put another class of work in them, be sure that He will not contradict Himself; He points you to the duty you have to do at home. If you have the idea that some work greater and holier than this has been entrusted to you, you are under a deception.

The Lord has not called you to neglect your home and your husband and children. He never works in this way; and He never will. Never for a moment suppose that God has given you a work that will necessitate a separation from your precious little flock. Do not leave them to become demoralized by improper associations and to harden their hearts against their mother. This is letting your light shine in a wrong way, altogether; you are making it more difficult for your children to become what God would have them and win heaven at last. God cares for them, and so must you if you claim to be His child.

During the first years of their lives is the time in which to work and watch and pray and encourage every good inclination. This work must go on without interruption. You may be urged to attend mothers' meetings and sewing circles, that you may do missionary work; but unless there is a faithful, understanding instructor to be left with your children, it is your duty to answer that the Lord has committed to you another work which you can in no wise neglect. You cannot overwork in any line without becoming disqualified for the work of training your little ones and making them what God would have them be. As Christ's co-worker you must bring them to Him disciplined and trained.

82

PROBLEMS OF MOTHERHOOD

Overcoming Circumstances: It is true that the wheels of domestic machinery will not always run smoothly; there is much to try the patience and tax the strength. But while mothers are not responsible for circumstances over which they have no control, it is useless to deny that circumstances make a great difference with mothers in their lifework. But their condemnation is when circumstances are allowed to rule and to subvert their principle, when they grow tired and unfaithful to their high trust and neglect their known duty.

The wife and mother who nobly overcomes difficulties under which others sink for want of patience and fortitude to persevere not only becomes strong herself in doing her duty, but her experience in overcoming temptations and obstacles qualifies her to be an efficient help to others, both by words and example. Many who do well under favorable circumstances seem to undergo a transformation of character under adversity and trial; they deteriorate in proportion to their troubles. God never designed that we should be the sport of circumstances.

Nourishing Discontent: Very many husbands and children who find nothing attractive at home, who are continually greeted by scolding and murmuring, seek comfort and amusement away from home.

The wife and mother, occupied with her household cares, frequently becomes thoughtless of the little courtesies that make home pleasant to the husband and children, even if she avoids dwelling upon her peculiar vexations and difficulties in their presence. While she is absorbed in preparing something to eat or to wear, the husband and sons go in and come out as strangers.

Assuming Unnecessary Burdens: Many mothers spend their time in doing needless nothings. They give their whole attention to the things of time and sense, and do not pause to think of the things of eternal interest. How many neglect their children, and the little ones grow up coarse, rough, and uncultivated!

If woman looks to God for strength and comfort and in His fear seeks to perform her daily duties, she will win the respect and confidence of her husband and see her children coming to maturity honorable men and women, having moral stamina to do right. But mothers who neglect present opportunities, and let their duties and burdens fall upon others, will find that their responsibility remains the same, and they will reap in bitterness what they have sown in carelessness and neglect. There is no chance work in this life; the harvest will be determined by the character of the seed sown.

MOTHER'S HEALTH AND APPEARANCE

Mother's Health to Be Cherished: The strength of the mother should be tenderly cherished. Instead of spending her precious strength in exhausting labor, her care and burdens should be lessened. Often the husband and father is unacquainted with the physical laws which the well-being of his family requires him to understand. Absorbed in the struggle for

85

a livelihood, or bent on acquiring wealth, and pressed with cares and perplexities, he allows to rest upon the wife and mother burdens that overtax her strength at the most critical period and cause feebleness and disease.

It is for her own interest, and that of her family, to save herself all unnecessary taxation and to use every means at her command to preserve life, health, and the energies which God has given her; for she will need the vigor of all her faculties for her great work. A portion of her time should be spent out of doors, in physical exercise, that she may be invigorated to do her work indoors with cheerfulness and thoroughness, being the light and blessing of the home.

Self-control in Diet: The mother needs the most perfect self-control; and in order to secure this, she should take all precautions against any physical or mental disorder. Her life should be ordered according to the laws of God and of health. As the diet materially affects the mind and disposition, she should be very careful in that particular, eating that which is nourishing but not stimulating, that her nerves may be calm and her temper equable. She will then find it easier to exercise patience in dealing with the varying tendencies of her children and to hold the reins of government firmly yet affectionately.

To Radiate Sunshine Under All Circumstances: The mother can and should do much toward controlling her nerves and mind when depressed; even when she is sick, she can, if she only schools herself, be pleasant and cheerful and can bear more noise than she would once have thought possible. She should not make the children feel her infirmities and cloud their young, sensitive minds by her depression of spirits, causing them to feel that the house is a tomb and the mother's room the most dismal place in the world.

Dress Attractively for Husband and Children: Some wives and mothers seem to think it is no matter how they look when about their work and when they are seen only by their husbands and children, but they are very particular to dress in taste for the eyes of those who have no special claims upon them. Is not the esteem and love of husband and children more to be prized than that of strangers or common friends? The happiness of husband and children should be more sacred to every wife and mother than that of all others.

Wear clothing that is becoming to you. This will increase the respect of your children for you. See to it that they, too, are dressed in a becoming manner. Do not allow them to fall into habits of untidiness.

Give Lessons in Neatness and Purity: If mothers allow themselves to wear untidy garments at home, they are teaching their children to follow in the same slovenly way. Many mothers think that anything is good enough for home wear, be it ever so soiled and shabby. But they soon lose their influence in the family. The children draw comparisons between their mother's dress and that of others who dress neatly, and their respect for her is weakened.

Mothers, make yourselves as attractive as possible, not by elaborate trimming, but by wearing clean, well-fitting garments. Thus you will give to your children constant lessons in neatness and purity. The love and respect of her children should be of the highest value to every mother. Everything upon her person should teach cleanliness and order and should be associated in their minds with purity.

There is a sense of fitness, an idea of the appropriateness of things, in the minds of even very young children; and how can they be impressed with the desirability of purity and holiness when their eyes daily rest on untidy dresses and disorderly rooms? How can the heavenly guests, whose home is where all is pure and holy, be invited into such a dwelling?

Order and cleanliness is the law of heaven; and in order to come into harmony with the divine arrangement, it is our duty to be neat.

THE CHILD

BEFORE BIRTH

Importance of Prenatal Influences: The effect of prenatal influences is by many parents looked upon as a matter of little moment; but heaven does not so regard it. The message sent by an angel of God, and twice given in the most solemn manner, shows it to be deserving of our most careful thought.

In the words spoken to the Hebrew mother [the wife of Manoah], God speaks to all mothers in every age. "Let her beware," the angel said; "all that I commanded her let her observe." The well-being of the child will be affected by the habits of the mother. Her appetites and passions are to be controlled by principle. There is something for her to shun, something for her to work against, if she fulfills God's purpose for her in giving her a child.

If before the birth of her child she is self-indulgent, if she is selfish, impatient, and exacting, these traits will be reflected in the disposition of the child. Thus many children have received as a birthright almost unconquerable tendencies to evil.

But if the mother unswervingly adheres to right principles, if she is temperate and self-denying, if she is kind, gentle, and unselfish, she may give her child these same precious traits of character.

Essentials of Prenatal Care: It is an error generally committed to make no difference in the life of a woman previous to the birth of her children. At this important period the labor of the mother should be lightened. Great changes are going on in her system. It requires a greater amount of blood, and therefore an increase of food of the most nourishing quality to convert into blood. Unless she has an abundant supply of nutritious food, she cannot retain her physical strength, and her offspring is robbed of vitality.

Her clothing also demands attention. Care should be taken to protect the body from a sense of chilliness. She should not call vitality unnecessarily to the surface to supply the want of sufficient clothing.

If the mother is deprived of an abundance of wholesome, nutritious food, she will lack in the quantity and quality of blood. Her circulation will be poor, and her child will lack in the very same things. There will be an inability in the offspring to appropriate food which it can convert into good blood to nourish the system.

The prosperity of mother and child depends much upon good, warm clothing and a supply of nourishing food.

Great care should be exercised to have the surroundings of the mother pleasant and happy. The husband and father is under special responsibility to do all in his power to lighten the burden of the wife and mother. He should bear, as much as possible, the burden of her condition. He should be affable, courteous, kind, and tender, and specially attentive to all her wants.

Appetite Alone Not a Safe Guide: The idea that women, because of their special condition, may let the appetite run riot is a mistake based on custom, but not on sound sense. The appetite of women in this condition may be variable, fitful, and difficult to gratify; and custom allows her to have anything she may fancy, without consulting reason as to whether such food can supply nutrition for her body and for the growth of her child. The food should be nutritious, but should not be of an exciting quality. If ever there is need of simplicity of diet and special care as to the quality of food eaten, it is in this important period.

Women who possess principle, and who are well instructed, will not depart from simplicity of diet at this time of all others. They will consider that another life is dependent upon them and will be careful in all their habits.

Self-control and Temperance: The mother's physical needs should in no case be neglected. Two lives are depending upon her, and her wishes should be tenderly regarded, her needs generously supplied. But at this time above all others she should avoid, in diet and in every other line, whatever would lessen physical or mental strength. By the command of God Himself she is placed under the most solemn obligation to exercise self-control.

The basis of a right character in the future man is made firm by habits of strict temperance in the mother prior to the birth of her child. This lesson should not be regarded with indifference.

A Peaceful, Trustful Attitude: She who expects to become a mother should keep her soul in the love of God. Her mind should be at peace; she should rest in the love of Jesus, practicing the words of Christ. She should remember that the mother is a laborer together with God.

CARE OF LITTLE CHILDREN

The Nursing Mother: The best food for the infant is the food that nature provides. Of this it should not be needlessly deprived. It is a heartless thing for a mother, for the sake of convenience or social enjoyment, to seek to free herself from the tender office of nursing her little one.

The character also of the child is more or less affected by the nature of the nourishment received from the mother. How important then that the mother, while nursing her infant, should preserve a happy state of mind, having the perfect control of her own spirit. By thus doing, the food of the child is not injured, and the calm, self-possessed course the mother pursues in the treatment of her child has very much to do in molding the mind of the infant. If it is nervous and easily agitated, the mother's careful, unhurried manner will have a soothing and correcting influence, and the health of the infant can be very much improved.

Food Is Not Attention: Infants have been greatly abused by improper treatment. If fretful, they have generally been fed to keep them quiet, when, in most cases, the very reason of their fretfulness was because of their having received too much food, made injurious by the wrong habits of the mother. More food only made the matter worse, for their stomachs were already overloaded.

Children are generally brought up from the cradle to indulge the appetite and are taught that they live to eat. The mother does much toward the formation of the character of her children in their childhood. She can teach them to control the appetite, or she can teach them to indulge the appetite and become gluttons.

The mother often arranges her plans to accomplish a certain amount through the day; and when the children trouble her, instead of taking time to soothe their little sorrows and divert them, something is given them to eat to keep them still, which answers the purpose for a short time but eventually makes things worse. The children's stomachs have been pressed with food, when they had not the least want of it.

All that was required was a little of the mother's time and attention. But she regarded her time as altogether too precious to devote to the amusement of the children. Perhaps the arrangement of her house in a tasteful manner for visitors to praise, and to have her food cooked in a fashionable style, are with her higher considerations than the happiness and health of her children.

Wholesome, Inviting, but Simple Food: Food should be so simple that its preparation will not absorb all the time of the mother. It is true, care should be taken to furnish the table with healthful food prepared in a wholesome and inviting manner. Do not think that anything you can carelessly throw together to serve as food is good enough for the children. But less time should be devoted to the preparation of unhealthful dishes for the table, to please a perverted taste, and more time to the education and training of the children.

Preparing the Baby's Layette: In the preparation of the baby's wardrobe, convenience, comfort, and health should be sought before fashion or a desire to excite admiration.

Cleanliness, Warmth, and Fresh Air: Babies require warmth, but a serious error is often committed in keeping them in overheated rooms, deprived to a great degree of fresh air.

The baby should be kept free from every influence that would tend to weaken or to poison the system. The most scrupulous care should be taken to have everything about it sweet and clean. While it may be necessary to protect the little ones from sudden or too great changes of temperature, care should be taken that, sleeping or waking, day or night, they breathe a pure, invigorating atmosphere.

Care of Sick Children: In many cases the sickness of children can be traced to errors in management. Irregularities in eating, insufficient clothing in the chilly evening, lack of vigorous exercise to keep the blood in healthy circulation, or lack of abundance of air for its purification may be the cause of the trouble. Let the parents study to find the causes of the sickness and then remedy the wrong conditions as soon as possible.

All parents have it in their power to learn much concerning the care and prevention, and even the treatment, of disease. Especially ought the mother to know what to do in common cases of illness in her family. She should know how to minister to her sick child. Her love and insight should fit her to perform services for it which could not so well be trusted to a stranger's hand.

MOTHER'S
FIRST DUTY

A Properly Trained Child: God sees all the possibilities in that mite of humanity. He sees that with proper training the child will become a power for good in the world. He watches with anxious interest to see whether the parents will carry out His plan or whether by mistaken kindness they will destroy His purpose, indulging the child to its present and eternal ruin. To transform this helpless and apparently insignificant being into a blessing to the world and an honor to God is a great and grand work. Parents should allow nothing to come between them and the obligation they owe to their children.

A Work for God and Country: Those who keep the law of God look upon their children with indefinable feelings of hope and fear, wondering what part they will act in the great conflict that is just before them. The anxious mother questions, "What stand will they take? What can I do to prepare them to act well their part, so that they will be the recipients of eternal glory?"

Great responsibilities rest upon you, mothers. Although you may not stand in national councils, you may do a great work for

God and your country. You may educate your children. You may aid them to develop characters that will not be swayed or influenced to do evil, but will sway and influence others to do right. By your fervent prayers of faith you can move the arm that moves the world.

Home Training Often Neglected: Notwithstanding boasted advancement that has been made in educational methods, the training of children at the present day is sadly defective. It is the home training that is neglected. Parents, and especially mothers, do not realize their responsibility. They have neither the patience to instruct nor the wisdom to control the little ones entrusted to their keeping.

It is too true that mothers are not standing at their post of duty, faithful to their motherhood. God requires of us nothing that we cannot in His strength perform, nothing that is not for our own good and the good of our children.

Seek Divine Aid: Did mothers but realize the importance of their mission, they would be much in secret prayer, presenting their children to Jesus, imploring His blessing upon them, and pleading for wisdom to discharge aright their sacred duties. Let the mother improve every opportunity to mold and fashion the disposition and habits of her children. Let her watch carefully the development of character, repressing traits that are too prominent, encouraging those that are deficient. Let her make her own life a pure and noble example to her precious charge.

The mother should enter upon her work with courage and energy, relying constantly upon divine aid in all her efforts. She should never rest satisfied until she sees in her children a gradual elevation of character, until they have a higher object in life than merely to seek their own pleasure.

The power of a mother's prayers cannot be too highly estimated. She who kneels beside her son and daughter through the vicissitudes of childhood, through the perils of youth, will never know till the judgment the influence of her prayers upon the life of her children. If she is connected by faith with the Son of God, the mother's tender hand may hold back her son from the power of temptation, may restrain her daughter from indulging in sin. When passion is warring for the mastery, the power of love, the restraining, earnest, determined influence of the mother, may balance the soul on the side of right.

Before visitors, before every other consideration, your children should come first. The labor due your child during its early years will admit of no neglect. There is no time in its life when the rule should be forgotten.

Do not send them out of doors that you may entertain your visitors, but teach them to be quiet and respectful in the presence of visitors.

Models of Goodness and Nobility: Mothers, be careful of your precious moments. Remember that your children are passing forward where they may be beyond your educating and training. You may be to them the very model of all that is good and pure and noble. Identify your interest with theirs.

Infant children are a mirror for the mother in which she may see reflected her own habits and deportment. How careful, then, should be her language and behavior in the presence of these little learners! Whatever traits of character she wishes to see developed in them she must cultivate in herself.

Joy of Work Satisfactorily Done: Children are the heritage of the Lord, and we are answerable to Him for our management of His property. The education and training of their children to be Christians is the highest service that parents can render to God. It is a work that demands patient labor—a lifelong, diligent, and persevering effort. By a neglect of this trust we prove ourselves unfaithful stewards.

In love, faith, and prayer let parents work for their households, until with joy they can come to God, saying, "Behold, I and the children whom the Lord hath given me."

ENCOURAGEMENT FOR MOTHERS

Jesus Blessed the Children: In the days of Christ mothers brought their children to Him, that He might lay His hands upon them in blessing. By this act they showed their faith in Jesus and the intense anxiety of their hearts for the present and future welfare of the little ones committed to their care. But the disciples could not see the need of interrupting the Master just for the sake of noticing the children, and as they were sending these mothers away, Jesus rebuked the disciples and commanded the crowd to make way for these faithful mothers with their little children. Said He, "Suffer little children, and forbid them not, to come unto me: for of such is the kingdom of heaven."

As the mothers passed along the dusty road and drew near the Saviour, He saw the unbidden tear and the quivering lip, as they offered a silent prayer in behalf of the children. He heard the words of rebuke from the disciples and promptly countermanded the order. His great heart of love was open to receive the children. One after another, He took them in His arms and blessed them, while one little child lay fast asleep, reclining against His bosom.

Jesus spoke words of encouragement to the mothers in reference to their work, and, oh, what a relief was thus brought to their minds! With what joy they dwelt upon the goodness and mercy of Jesus, as they looked back to that memorable occasion! His gracious words had removed the burden from their hearts and inspired them with fresh hope and courage. All sense of weariness was gone.

This is an encouraging lesson to mothers for all time. After they have done the best they can do for the good of their children, they may bring them to Jesus. Even the babes in the mother's arms are precious in His sight. And as the mother's heart yearns for the help she knows she cannot give, the grace she cannot bestow, and she casts herself and children into the merciful arms of Christ, He will receive and bless them; He will give peace, hope, and happiness to mother and children. This is a precious privilege which Jesus has granted to all mothers.

Let mothers come to Jesus with their perplexities. They will find grace sufficient to aid them in the management of their children. The gates are open for every mother who would lay her burdens at the Saviour's feet. He still invites the mothers to lead up their little ones to be blessed by Him. Even the babe in its mother's arms may dwell under the shadow of the Almighty through the faith of the praying mother. John the Baptist was filled with the Holy Spirit from his birth. If we live in communion with God, we too may expect the divine Spirit to mold our little ones, even from their earliest moments.

Young Hearts Are Susceptible: He [Christ] identified Himself with the lowly, the needy, and the afflicted. He took little children in His arms and descended to the level of the young. His large heart of love could comprehend their trials and necessities, and He enjoyed their happiness. His spirit, wearied with the bustle and confusion of the crowded city, tired of association with crafty and hypocritical men, found rest and peace in the society of innocent children. His presence never repulsed them. The Majesty of heaven condescended to answer their questions and simplified His important lessons to meet their childish understanding. He planted in their young, expanding minds the seeds of truth that would spring up and produce a plentiful harvest in their riper years.

"Suffer the little children to come unto me, and forbid them not: for of such is the kingdom of heaven." These precious words are to be cherished, not only by every mother, but by every father as well. These words are an encouragement to parents to press their children into His notice, to ask in the name of Christ that the Father may let His blessing rest upon their entire family. Not only are the best beloved to receive particular attention, but also the restless, wayward children, who need careful training and tender guidance.

TRUE ESTIMATE OF CHILDREN

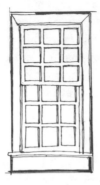

Purchased by Christ: Christ placed such a high estimate upon your children that He gave His life for them. Treat them as the purchase of His blood. Patiently and firmly train them for Him. Discipline with love and forbearance. As you do this, they will become a crown of rejoicing to you and will shine as lights in the world.

The youngest child that loves and fears God is greater in His sight than the most talented and learned man who neglects the great salvation. The youth who consecrate their hearts and lives to God have, in so doing, placed themselves in connection with the Fountain of all wisdom and excellence.

As Precious As the Angels: The soul of the little child that believes in Christ is as precious in His sight as are the angels about His throne. They are to be brought to Christ and trained for Christ. They are to be guided in the path of obedience, not indulged in appetite or vanity.

God's Property Entrusted to Parents: Children derive life and being from their parents, and yet it is through the creative power of God that your children have life, for God is the Life-giver. Let it be remembered that children are not to be treated as though they were our own personal property. Children are the heritage of the Lord, and the plan of redemption includes their salvation as well as ours. They have been entrusted to parents in order that they might be brought up in the nurture and admonition of the Lord, that they might be qualified to do their work in time and eternity.

Mothers, deal gently with your little ones. Christ was once a little child. For His sake honor the children. Look upon them as a sacred charge, not to be indulged, petted, and idolized, but to be taught to live pure, noble lives. They are God's property; He loves them, and calls upon you to cooperate with Him in helping them to form perfect characters.

The youth need to be impressed with the truth that their endowments are not their own. Strength, time, intellect, are but lent treasures. They belong to God, and it should be the resolve of every youth to put them to the highest use. He is a branch, from which God expects fruit; a steward, whose capital must yield increase; a light, to illuminate the world's darkness. Every youth, every child, has a work to do for the honor of God and the uplifting of humanity.

Path of Life for Children: Jesus knows our infirmities and has Himself shared our experience in all things but in sin; therefore He has prepared for us a path suited to our strength and capacity and, like Jacob, has marched softly and in evenness with the children as they were able to endure, that He might entertain us by the comfort of His company and be to us a perpetual guide. He does not despise, neglect, or leave behind the children of the flock. He has not bidden us move forward and leave them. He has not traveled so hastily as to leave us with our children behind. Oh, no; but He has evened the path to life, even for children. And parents are required in His name to lead them along the narrow way. God has appointed us a path suited to the strength and capacity of children.

MOTHER'S HELPERS

Children to Be Partners: Children as well as parents have important duties in the home. They should be taught that they are a part of the home firm. They are fed and clothed and loved and cared for; and they should respond to these many mercies by bearing their share of the home burdens and bringing all the happiness possible into the family of which they are members.

Let the children know that they are helping father and mother by doing little errands. Give them some work to do for you, and tell them that afterward they can have a time to play.

Children have active minds, and they need to be employed in lifting the burdens of practical life. They should never be left to pick up their own employment. Parents should control this matter themselves.

Everyone Has Obligations: Parents are under obligation to feed and clothe and educate their children, and children are under obligation to serve their parents with cheerful, earnest fidelity. When children cease to feel their obligation to share the toil and burden with their parents, then how would it suit them to have their parents cease to feel their obligation to provide for them? In ceasing to do the duties that devolve upon them to be useful to their parents, to lighten their burdens by doing that which may be disagreeable and full of toil, children miss their opportunity of obtaining a most valuable education that will fit them for future usefulness.

There is nothing which more surely leads to evil than to lift all burdens from children, leaving them to an idle, aimless life, to do nothing, or to occupy themselves as they please. The minds of children are active, and if not occupied with that which is good and useful, they will inevitably turn to what is bad. While it is right and necessary for them to have recreation, they should be taught to work, to have regular hours for physical labor and also for reading and study. See that they have employment suited to their years.

Children Should Learn to Bear Burdens: Parents should awaken to the fact that the most important lesson for their children to learn is that they must act their part in bearing the burdens of the home. Parents should teach their children to take a common-sense view of life, to realize that they are to be useful in the world. In the home, under the supervision of a wise

103

mother, boys and girls should receive their first instruction in bearing the burdens of life.

Children Enjoy Simple Tasks: Children can be educated to be helpful. They are naturally active and inclined to be busy; and this activity is susceptible of being trained and directed in the right channel. Children may be taught, when young, to lift daily their light burdens, each child having some particular task for the accomplishment of which he is responsible to his parents or guardian. They will thus learn to bear the yoke of duty while young; and the performance of their little tasks will become a pleasure, bringing them a happiness that is only gained by well-doing. They will become accustomed to work and responsibility and will relish employment, perceiving that life holds for them more important business than that of amusing themselves.

Work is good for children; they are happier to be usefully employed a large share of the time; their innocent amusements are enjoyed with a keener zest after the successful completion of their tasks. Labor strengthens both the muscles and the mind. Children that are properly trained, as they advance in years, learn to love that labor which makes the burdens of their friends lighter.

Assures Mental Balance: In the fulfillment of their apportioned tasks strength of memory and a right balance of mind may be gained, as well as stability of character and dispatch. The day, with its round of little duties, calls for thought, calculation, and a plan of action. As the children become older, still more can be required of them. It should not be exhaustive labor, nor should their work be so protracted as to fatigue and discourage them; but it should be judiciously selected with reference to the physical development most desirable and the proper cultivation of the mind and character.

Strengthens Home Ties: In the home training of the youth the principle of cooperation is invaluable. The older ones should be their parents' assistants, entering into their plans and sharing their responsibilities and burdens. Let fathers and mothers take time to teach their children; let them show that they value their help, desire their confidence, and enjoy their companionship; and the children will not be slow to respond. Not only will the parents' burden be lightened, and the children receive a practical training of inestimable worth, but there will be a strengthening of the home ties and a deepening of the very foundations of character.

Growth in Mental, Moral, Spiritual Excellence: Children and youth should take pleasure in making lighter the cares of father and mother, showing an unselfish interest in the home. As they cheerfully lift the burdens that fall to their share, they are receiving a training which will fit them for positions of trust and usefulness. Each year they are to make steady advancement, gradually but surely laying aside the inexperience of boyhood and girlhood for the experience of manhood and womanhood. In the faithful performance of the simple duties of the home, boys and girls lay the foundation for mental, moral, and spiritual excellence.

It is a sin to let children grow up in idleness. Let them exercise their limbs and muscles, even if it wearies them. If they are not overworked, how can weariness harm them more than it harms you? There is quite a difference between weariness and exhaustion. Children need more frequent change of employment and intervals of rest than grown persons do; but even when quite young, they may begin learning to work, and they will be happy in the thought that they are making themselves useful. Their sleep will be sweet after healthful labor, and they will be refreshed for the next day's work.

Do Not Say, "My Children Bother Me": "Oh," say some mothers, "my children bother me when they try to help me." So did mine, but do you think I let them know it? Praise your children. Teach them, line upon line, precept upon precept.

HONOR DUE PARENTS

Indebted to Parents: Children should feel that they are indebted to their parents, who have watched over them in infancy and nursed them in sickness. They should realize that their parents have suffered much anxiety on their account.

Children, when they become of age, will prize the parent who labored faithfully, and would not permit them to cherish wrong feelings or indulge in evil habits.

A Command Binding on All: "Honour thy father and thy mother: that thy days may be long upon the land which the Lord thy God giveth thee." This is the first commandment with promise. It is binding upon childhood and youth, upon the middle-aged and the aged. There is no period in life when children are excused from honoring their parents.

Parents are entitled to a degree of love and respect which is due to no other person. God Himself, who has placed upon them a responsibility for the souls committed to their charge, has ordained that during the earlier years of life parents shall stand in the place of God to their children. And he who rejects the rightful authority of his parents is rejecting the authority of God. The fifth commandment requires children not only to yield respect, submission, and obedience to their parents, but also to give them love and tenderness, to lighten their cares, to guard their reputation, and to succor and comfort them in old age.

In this rebellious age children who have not received right instruction and discipline have but little sense of their obligations to their parents. It is often the case that the more their parents do for them, the more ungrateful they are and the less they respect them. Children who have been petted and waited upon always expect it; and if their expectations are not met, they are disappointed and discouraged.

This same disposition will be seen through their whole lives; they will be helpless, leaning upon others for aid, expecting others to favor them and yield to them. And if they are opposed, even after they have grown to manhood and womanhood, they think themselves abused; and thus they worry their way through the world, hardly able to bear their own weight, often murmuring and fretting because everything does not suit them.

Show Your Love: I have seen children who seemed to have no affection to give to their parents, no expressions of love and endearment, which are due them and which they would appreciate; but they lavish an abundance of affection and caresses to select ones for whom they show preference. Is this as God would have it? No, no.

Bring all the rays of sunshine, of love, and of affection into the home circle. Your father and mother will appreciate these little attentions you can give. Your efforts to lighten the burdens, and to repress every word of fretfulness and ingratitude, show that you are not a thoughtless child, and that you do appreciate the care and love that has been bestowed upon you in the years of your helpless infancy and childhood.

107

COUNSEL  TO CHILDREN

Seek God Early: Children and youth should begin early to seek God; for early habits and impressions will frequently exert a powerful influence upon the life and character. Therefore the youth who would be like Samuel, John, and especially like Christ, must be faithful in the things which are least, turning away from the companions who plan evil and who think that their life in the world is to be one of pleasure and selfish indulgence.

Many of the little home duties are overlooked as of no consequence; but if the small things are neglected, the larger duties will be also. You want to be whole men and women, with pure, sound, noble characters. Begin the work at home; take up the little duties and do them with thoroughness and exactness. When the Lord sees you are faithful in that which is least, He will entrust you with larger responsibilities. Be careful how you build, and what kind of material you put into the building. The characters you are now forming will be lasting as eternity.

Let Jesus take possession of your mind, your heart, and your affections; and work as Christ worked, doing conscientiously the home duties, little acts of self-denial and deeds of kindness, employing the moments diligently, keeping a careful watch against little sins and a grateful heart for little blessings, and you will have at last such a testimony for yourself as was given of John and Samuel, and especially of Christ: "And Jesus increased in wisdom and stature, and in favor with God and man."

An Individual Choice: Watch and pray, and obtain a personal experience in the things of God. Your parents may teach you, they may try to guide your feet into safe paths; but it is impossible for them to change your heart. You must give your heart to Jesus and walk in the precious light of truth that He has given you. Faithfully take up your duties in the homelife, and, through the grace of God, you may grow up unto the full stature of what Christ would have a child grow to be in Him.

In childhood and youth you may have an experience in the service of God. Do the things that you know to be right. Be obedient to your parents. Listen to their counsels; for if they love and fear God, upon them will be laid the responsibility of educating, disciplining, and training your soul for the immortal life. Thankfully receive the help they want to give you, and make their hearts glad by cheerfully submitting yourselves to the dictates of their wiser judgments. In this way you will honor your parents, glorify God, and become a blessing to those with whom you associate.

Pray for Help: Children should pray for grace to resist the temptations which will come to them—temptations to have their

109

own way and to do their own selfish pleasure. As they ask Christ to help them in their life service to be truthful, kind, obedient, and to bear their responsibilities in the family circle, He will hear their simple prayer.

Jesus would have the children and the youth come to Him with the same confidence with which they go to their parents. As a child asks his mother or father for bread when he is hungry, so the Lord would have you ask Him for the things which you need.

Jesus knows the needs of children, and He loves to listen to their prayers. Let the children shut out the world and everything that would attract the thoughts from God; and let them feel that they are alone with God, that His eye looks into the inmost heart and reads the desire of the soul, and that they may talk with God.

Then, children, ask God to do for you those things that you cannot do for yourselves. Tell Jesus everything. Lay open before Him the secrets of your heart; for His eye searches the inmost recesses of the soul, and He reads your thoughts as an open book. When you have asked for the things that are necessary for your soul's good, believe that you receive them, and you shall have them.

Many children go about their home duties as though they were disagreeable tasks, and their faces plainly show the disagreeable. They find fault and murmur, and nothing is done willingly. This is not Christlike; it is the spirit of Satan, and if you cherish it, you will be like him. You will be miserable yourselves and will make all about you miserable.

Do not complain of how much you have to do and how little time you have for amusement, but be thoughtful and caretaking. By employing your time in some useful work, you will be closing a door against Satan's temptations. Remember that Jesus lived not to please Himself, and you must be like Him. Make this matter one of religious principle, and ask Jesus to help you. By exercising your mind in this direction, you will be preparing to become burden bearers in the cause of God as you have been caretakers in the home circle. You will have a good influence upon others and may win them to the service of Christ.

God's Reward for the Daniels of Today: There is now need of men who, like Daniel, will do and dare. A pure heart and a strong, fearless hand are wanted in the world today. God designed that man should be constantly improving, daily reaching a higher point in the scale of excellence. He will help us if we seek to help ourselves. Our hope of happiness in two worlds depends upon our improvement in one.

Dear youth, God calls upon you to do a work which through His grace you can do. "Present your bodies a living sacrifice, holy, acceptable unto God, which is your reasonable service." Stand forth in your God-given manhood and womanhood. Show a purity of tastes, appetite, and habits that bears comparison with Daniel's. God will reward you with calm nerves, a clear brain, an unimpaired judgment, keen perceptions. The youth of today whose principles are firm and unwavering will be blessed with health of body, mind, and soul.

Begin Now: The youth are now deciding their own eternal destiny, and I would appeal to you to consider the commandment to which God has annexed such a promise, "That thy days may be long upon the land which the Lord thy God giveth thee." Children, do you desire eternal life? Then respect and honor your parents. Do not wound and grieve their hearts and cause them to spend sleepless nights in anxiety and distress over your case. If you have sinned in not rendering love and obedience to them, begin now to redeem the past. You cannot afford to take any other course, for it means to you the loss of eternal life.

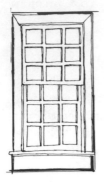

HOME GOVERNMENT

The Guiding Principle: Fathers and mothers should make it their life study that their children may become as nearly perfect in character as human effort, combined with divine aid, can make them. This work, with all its importance and responsibility, they have accepted, in that they have brought children into the world.

Necessary Rules: Every Christian home should have rules; and parents should, in their words and in their deportment toward each other, give to the children a precious living example of what they desire them to be. Teach the children and youth to respect themselves, to be true to God, true to principle; teach them to respect and obey the law of God. Then these principles will control their lives and will be carried out in their association with others.

God Himself established the family relations. His Word is the only safe guide in the management of children. Human philosophy has not discovered more than God knows or devised a wiser plan of dealing with children than that given by our Lord. Who can better understand all the needs of children than their Creator? Who can feel a deeper interest in their welfare than He who bought them with His own blood? If the Word of God were carefully studied and faithfully obeyed, there would be less soul anguish over the perverse conduct of wicked children.

Respect the Children's Rights: Remember that children have rights which must be respected.

Children have claims which their parents should acknowledge and respect. They have a right to such an education and training as will make them useful, respected, and beloved members of society here, and give them a moral fitness for the society of the pure and holy hereafter. The young should be taught that both their present and their future well-being depend to a great degree on the habits they form in childhood and youth. They should be early accustomed to submission, self-denial, and a regard for others' happiness. They should be taught to subdue the hasty temper, to withhold the passionate word, to manifest unvarying kindness, courtesy, and self-control.

Neither Blind Affection nor Undue Severity: While we are not to indulge blind affection, neither are we to manifest undue severity. Children cannot be brought to the Lord by force. They can be led, but not driven. "My sheep hear my voice, and I know

113

them, and they follow me," Christ declares. He did not say, My sheep hear My voice and are forced into the path of obedience. In the government of children love must be shown. Never should parents cause their children pain by harshness or unreasonable exactions. Harshness drives souls into Satan's net.

Harshness Not Required: Let none imagine that harshness and severity are necessary to secure obedience. I have seen the most efficient family government maintained without a harsh word or look. I have been in other families where commands were constantly given in an authoritative tone, and harsh rebukes and severe punishments were often administered. In the first case the children followed the course pursued by the parents and seldom spoke to one another in harsh tones. In the second also the parental example was imitated by the children; and cross words, faultfindings, and disputes were heard from morning till night.

Harsh words sour the temper and wound the hearts of children, and in some cases these wounds are difficult to heal. Children are sensitive to the least injustice, and some become discouraged under it and will neither heed the loud, angry voice of command nor care for threatenings of punishment.

There is danger of too severely criticizing small things. Criticism that is too severe, rules that are too rigid, lead to the disregard of all regulations; and by and by children thus educated will show the same disrespect for the laws of Christ.

Uniform Firmness, Unimpassioned Control: Children have sensitive, loving natures. They are easily pleased and easily made unhappy. By gentle discipline in loving words and acts mothers may bind their children to their hearts. To manifest severity and to be exacting with children are great mistakes. Uniform firmness and unimpassioned control are necessary to the discipline of every family. Say what you mean calmly, move with consideration, and carry out what you say without deviation.

It will pay to manifest affection in your association with your

114

children. Do not repel them by lack of sympathy in their childish sports, joys, and griefs. Never let a frown gather upon your brow or a harsh word escape your lips. God writes all these words in His book of records.

Unsteadiness in family government is productive of great harm, in fact is nearly as bad as no government at all. The question is often asked, Why are the children of religious parents so often headstrong, defiant, and rebellious? The reason is to be found in the home training. Too often the parents are not united in their family government.

A fitful government—at one time holding the lines firmly, and at another allowing that which has been condemned—is ruination to a child.

Rules for Both Parents and Children: God is our Lawgiver and King, and parents are to place themselves under His rule. This rule forbids all oppression from parents and all disobedience from children. The Lord is full of lovingkindness, mercy, and truth. His law is holy, just, and good, and must be obeyed by parents and children.

The rules which should regulate the lives of parents and children flow from a heart of infinite love, and God's rich blessing will rest upon those parents who administer His law in their homes, and upon the children who obey this law. The combined influence of mercy and justice is to be felt. "Mercy and truth are met together; righteousness and peace have kissed each other." Households under this discipline will walk in the way of the Lord, to do justice and judgment.

A UNITED FRONT

Parents Must Work Together: Parents are to work together as a unit. There must be no division. But many parents work at cross-purposes, and thus the children are spoiled by mismanagement.

It sometimes happens that, of the mother and father, one is too indulgent and the other too severe. This difference works against good results in the formation of the characters of their children. No harsh force is to be exercised in carrying out reforms, but at the same time no weak indulgence must be shown. The mother is not to seek to blind the eyes of the father to the faults of the children, neither is she to influence them to do those things which the father has forbidden them to do. Not one seed of doubt should the mother plant in her children's minds in regard to the wisdom of the father's management. She should not, by her course of action, counteract the work of the father.

If fathers and mothers are at variance, one working against the other to counteract each other's influence, the family will be in a demoralized condition, and neither the father nor the mother will receive the respect and confidence that are essential to a well-governed family. Children are quick to discern anything that will cast a reflection upon the rules and regulations of a household, especially those regulations that restrict their actions.

Lessons in Deception: Some fond mothers suffer wrongs in their children which should not be allowed in them for a moment. The wrongs of the children are sometimes concealed from the father. Articles of dress or some other indulgence is granted by the mother with the understanding that the father is to know nothing about it, for he would reprove for these things.

Here a lesson of deception is effectually taught the children. Then if the father discovers these wrongs, excuses are made and but half the truth told. The mother is not openhearted. She does not consider as she should that the father has the same interest in the children as herself, and that he should not be kept ignorant of the wrongs or besetments that ought to be corrected in them while young. Things have been covered. The children know the lack of union in their parents, and it has its effect. The children begin young to deceive, cover up, tell things in a different light from what they are to their mother as well as their father. Exaggeration becomes habit, and blunt falsehoods come to be told with but little conviction or reproof of conscience.

These wrongs commenced by the mother's concealing things from the father, who has an equal interest with her in the character their children are forming. The father should have been consulted freely. All should have been laid open to him. But the opposite course, taken to conceal the wrongs of the children, encourages in them a disposition to deceive, a lack of truthfulness and honesty.

There should always be a fixed principle with Christian parents to be united in the government of their children. There is a fault in this respect with some parents—a lack of union. The fault is sometimes with the father, but oftener with the mother. The fond mother pets and indulges her children. The father's labor calls him from home often, and from the society of his children. The mother's influence tells. Her example does much toward forming the character of the children.

Confusing the Children: The family firm must be well organized. Together the father and mother must consider their responsibilities, and with a clear comprehension undertake their task. There is to be no variance. The father and mother should never in the presence of their children criticize each other's plans and judgment.

If parents do not agree, let them absent themselves from the presence of their children until an understanding can be arrived at.

Too often the parents are not united in their family government. The father, who is with his children but little, and is ignorant of their peculiarities of disposition and temperament, is harsh and severe. He does not control his temper, but corrects in passion. The child knows this, and instead of being subdued, the punishment fills him with anger. The mother allows misdemeanors to pass at one time for which she will severely punish at another. The children never know just what to expect, and are tempted to see how far they can transgress with impunity. Thus are sown seeds of evil that spring up and bear fruit.

If parents are united in this work of discipline, the child will understand what is required of him. But if the father, by word or look, shows that he does not approve of the discipline the mother gives; if he feels that she is too strict and thinks that he must make up for the harshness by petting and indulgence, the child will be ruined. He will soon learn that he can do as he pleases. Parents who commit this sin against their children are accountable for the ruin of their souls.

Much Prayer and Sober Reflection: Affection cannot be lasting, even in the home circle, unless there is a conformity of the will and disposition to the will of God. All the faculties and passions are to be brought into harmony with the attributes of Jesus Christ. If the father and mother in the love and fear of God unite their interests to have authority in the home, they will see the necessity of much prayer, much sober reflection. And as they seek God, their eyes will be opened to see heavenly messengers present to protect them in answer to the prayer of faith. They will overcome the weakness of their character and go on unto perfection.

The Silken Cord of Love: Father and mother, bind your hearts in closest, happiest union. Do not grow apart, but bind yourselves more closely to each other; then you are prepared to bind your children's hearts to you by the silken cord of love.

RELIGION IN THE FAMILY

Make Religion Real: Family religion consists in bringing up the children in the nurture and admonition of the Lord. Everyone in the family is to be nourished by the lessons of Christ, and the interest of each soul is to be strictly guarded, in order that Satan shall not deceive and allure away from Christ. This is the standard every family should aim to reach, and they should determine not to fail or to be discouraged. When parents are diligent and vigilant in their instruction, and train their children with an eye single to the glory of God, they cooperate with God, and God cooperates with them in the saving of the souls of the children for whom Christ has died.

Religious instruction means much more than ordinary instruction. It means that you are to pray with your children, teaching them how to approach Jesus and tell Him all their wants. It means that you are to show in your life that Jesus is everything to you, and that His love makes you patient, kind, forbearing, and yet firm in commanding your children after you, as did Abraham.

If fathers and mothers are true Christians in the family, they will be useful members of the church and be able to conduct affairs in the church and in society after the same manner in which they conduct their family concerns. Parents, let not your religion be simply a profession, but let it become a reality.

Where religion is a practical thing in the home, great good is accomplished. Religion will lead the parents to do the very work God designed should be done in the home. Children will be brought up in the fear and admonition of the Lord.

If religion is to influence society, it must first influence the home circle. If children were trained to love and fear God at home, when they go forth into the world, they would be prepared to train their own families for God, and thus the principles of truth would become implanted in society and would exert a telling influence in the world. Religion should not be divorced from home education.

Home Religion Is Most Important: In the home the foundation is laid for the prosperity of the church. The influences that rule in the homelife are carried into the church life; therefore church duties should first begin in the home.

When we have good home religion, we will have excellent meeting religion. Hold the fort at home. Consecrate your family

121

to God, and then speak and act at home as a Christian. Be kind and forbearing and patient at home, knowing that you are teachers. Every mother is a teacher, and every mother should be a learner in the school of Christ that she may know how to teach, that she may give the right mold, the right form of character to her children.

Mistake to Delay Religious Instruction: Parents make a most terrible mistake when they neglect the work of giving their children religious training, thinking that they will come out all right in the future and, as they get older, will of themselves be anxious for a religious experience. Cannot you see, parents, that if you do not plant the precious seeds of truth, of love, of heavenly attributes, in the heart, Satan will sow the field of the heart with tares?

Too often children are allowed to grow up without religion because their parents think they are too young to have Christian duties enjoined upon them.

The question of the duty of children in regard to religious matters is to be decided absolutely and without hesitancy while they are members of the family.

Parents, what course are you pursuing? Are you acting upon the idea that in religious matters your children should be left free of all restraint? Are you leaving them without counsel or admonition through childhood and youth? Are you leaving them to do as they please? If so, you are neglecting your God-given responsibilities.

Adapt Instruction to the Child's Age: As soon as the little ones are intelligent to understand, parents should tell them the story of Jesus that they may drink in the precious truth concerning the Babe of Bethlehem. Impress upon the children's minds sentiments of simple piety that are adapted to their years and ability. Bring your children in prayer to Jesus, for He has made it possible for them to learn religion as they learn to frame the words of the language.

When very young, children are susceptible to divine influences. The Lord takes these children under His special care; and when they are brought up in the nurture and admonition of the Lord, they are a help and not a hindrance to their parents.

Parents Jointly Foster Religion: The father and the mother are responsible for the maintenance of religion in the home.

Let not the mother gather to herself so many cares that she cannot give time to the spiritual needs of her family. Let parents seek God for guidance in their work. On their knees before Him they will gain a true understanding of their great responsibilities, and there they can commit their children to One who will never err in counsel and instruction.

The father of the family should not leave to the mother all the care of imparting spiritual instruction. A large work is to be done by fathers and mothers, and both should act their individual part in preparing their children for the grand review of the judgment.

Children Look to Parents for Consistent Life: Everything leaves its impress upon the youthful mind. The countenance is studied, the voice has its influence, and the deportment is closely imitated by them. Fretful and peevish fathers and mothers are giving their children lessons which at some period in their lives they would give all the world, were it theirs, could they unlearn. Children must see in the lives of their parents that consistency which is in accordance with their faith. By leading a consistent life and exercising self-control, parents may mold the characters of their children.

God Honors a Well-ordered Family: Fathers and mothers who make God first in their households, who teach their children that the fear of the Lord is the beginning of wisdom, glorify God before angels and before men by presenting to the world a well-ordered, well-disciplined family, a family that love and obey God instead of rebelling against Him. Christ is not a stranger in their homes; His name is a household name, revered and glorified. Angels delight in a home where God reigns supreme and the children are taught to reverence religion, the Bible, and their Creator. Such families can claim the promise: "Them that honour me I will honour."

Parents are not to compel their children to have a form of religion, but they are to place eternal principles before them in an attractive light.

Parents are to make the religion of Christ attractive by their cheerfulness, their Christian courtesy, and their tender, compassionate sympathy; but they are to be firm in requiring respect and obedience. Right principles must be established in the mind of the child.

Why Some Parents Fail: Some parents, although they profess to be religious, do not keep before their children the fact that God is to be served and obeyed, that convenience, pleasure, or inclination should not interfere with His claims upon them. "The fear of the Lord is the beginning of wisdom." This fact should be woven into the very life and character. The right conception of God through the knowledge of Christ, who died that we might be saved, should be impressed upon their minds.

You may think, parents, that you have not time to do all this, but you must take time to do your work in your family, else Satan will supply the deficiency. Cut out everything else from your life that prevents this work from being done, and train your children after His order. Neglect anything of a temporal nature, be satisfied to live economically, bind about your wants, but for Christ's sake do not neglect the religious training of yourselves and your children.

MORAL STANDARDS

Prevalence of Immorality: Immorality abounds everywhere. Licentiousness is the special sin of this age. Never did vice lift its deformed head with such boldness as now. The people seem to be benumbed, and the lovers of virtue and true goodness are nearly discouraged by its boldness, strength, and prevalence. The iniquity which abounds is not merely confined to the unbeliever and the scoffer. Would that this were the case, but it is not. Many men and women who profess the religion of Christ are guilty. Even some who profess to be looking for His appearing are no more prepared for that event than Satan himself. They are not cleansing themselves from all pollution.

They have so long served their lust that it is natural for their thoughts to be impure and their imaginations corrupt. It is as impossible to cause their minds to dwell upon pure and holy things as it would be to turn the course of Niagara and send its waters pouring up the falls. Every Christian will have to learn to restrain his passions and be controlled by principle. Unless he does this, he is unworthy of the Christian name.

Lovesick sentimentalism prevails. Married men receive attention from married or unmarried women; women also appear to be charmed and lose reason and spiritual discernment and good common sense; they do the very things that the Word of God condemns. It is like an infatuating game at which they are playing. Satan leads them on to ruin themselves, to imperil the cause of God, to crucify the Son of God afresh and put Him to an open shame.

Ignorance, pleasure loving, and sinful habits, corrupting soul, body, and spirit, make the world full of moral leprosy; a deadly moral malaria is destroying thousands and tens of thousands. What shall be done to save our youth? We can do little, but God lives and reigns, and He can do much.

Contrast to the World: The liberties taken in this age of corruption should be no criterion for Christ's followers. These fashionable exhibitions of familiarity should not exist among Christians fitting for immortality. If lasciviousness, pollution, adultery, crime, and murder are the order of the day among those who know not the truth, and who refuse to be controlled by the principles of God's Word, how important that the class professing to be followers of Christ, closely allied to God and angels, should show them a better and nobler way! How important that by their chastity and virtue they stand in marked contrast to that class who are controlled by brute passions!

Live Above Reproach: The mind of a man or woman does not come down in a moment from purity and holiness to depravity, corruption, and crime. It takes time to transform the human to the divine, or to degrade those formed in the image of God to the brutal or the satanic. By beholding we become changed.

Though formed in the image of his Maker, man can so educate his mind that sin which he once loathed will become pleasant to him. As he ceases to watch and pray, he ceases to guard the citadel, the heart, and engages in sin and crime. The mind is debased, and it is impossible to elevate it from corruption while it is being educated to enslave the moral and intellectual powers and bring them in subjection to grosser passions. Constant war against the carnal mind must be maintained; and we must be aided by the refining influence of the grace of God, which will attract the mind upward and habituate it to meditate upon pure and holy things.

Uphold High Standards: I write with a distressed heart that the women in this age, both married and unmarried, too frequently do not maintain the reserve that is necessary. They act like coquettes. They encourage the attentions of single and married men, and those who are weak in moral power will be ensnared.

These things, if allowed, deaden the moral senses and blind the mind so that crime does not appear sinful. Thoughts are awakened that would not have been if woman had kept her place in all modesty and sobriety. She may have had no unlawful purpose or motive herself, but she has given encouragement to men who are tempted, and who need all the help they can get from those associated with them. By being circumspect, reserved, taking no liberties, receiving no unwarrantable attentions, but preserving a high moral tone and becoming dignity, much evil might be avoided.

Women are too often tempters. On one pretense or another they engage the attention of men, married or unmarried, and lead them on till they transgress the law of God, till their usefulness is ruined, and their souls are in jeopardy.

A woman who will allow an unchaste word or hint to be uttered in her presence is not as God would have her; one that will permit any undue familiarity or impure suggestion does not

127

preserve her godlike womanhood.

Control Your Thoughts: You should control your thoughts. This will not be an easy task; you cannot accomplish it without close and even severe effort. Yet God requires this of you; it is a duty resting upon every accountable being. You are responsible to God for your thoughts. If you indulge in vain imaginations, permitting your mind to dwell upon impure subjects, you are, in a degree, as guilty before God as if your thoughts were carried into action. All that prevents the action is the lack of opportunity.

Be Faithful to Marriage Vows: How careful should the husband and father be to maintain his loyalty to his marriage vows! How circumspect should be his character, lest he shall encourage thoughts in young girls, or even in married women, that are not in accordance with the high, holy standard—the commandments of God! Those commandments Christ shows to be exceedingly broad, reaching even the thoughts, intents, and purposes of the heart. Here is where many are delinquent. Their heart imaginings are not of the pure, holy character which God requires; and however high their calling, however talented they may be, God will mark iniquity against them and will count them as far more guilty and deserving of His wrath than those who have less talent, less light, less influence.

Maintain Family Privacy: Oh, how many lives are made bitter by the breaking down of the walls which enclose the privacies of every family, and which are calculated to preserve its purity and sanctity! A third person is taken into the confidence of the wife, and her private family matters are laid open before the special friend. This is the device of Satan to estrange the hearts of the husband and wife. Oh, that this would cease! What a world of trouble would be saved! Lock within your own hearts the knowledge of each other's faults. Tell your troubles alone to God. He can give you right counsel and sure consolation which will be pure, having no bitterness in it.

DIVORCE

A Contract for Life: In the youthful mind marriage is clothed with romance, and it is difficult to divest it of this feature, with which imagination covers it, and to impress the mind with a sense of the weighty responsibilities involved in the marriage vow. This vow links the destinies of the two individuals with bonds which naught but the hand of death should sever.

Every marriage engagement should be carefully considered, for marriage is a step taken for life. Both the man and the woman should carefully consider whether they can cleave to each other through the vicissitudes of life as long as they both shall live.

Misconceptions of Marriage: Among the Jews a man was permitted to put away his wife for the most trivial offenses, and the woman was then at liberty to marry again. This practice led to great wretchedness and sin. In the Sermon on the Mount Jesus declared plainly that there could be no dissolution of the marriage tie except for unfaithfulness to the marriage vow. "Every one," He said, "that putteth away his wife, saving for the cause of fornication, maketh her an adulteress: and whosoever shall marry her when she is put away committeth adultery."

Jesus came to our world to rectify mistakes and to restore the moral image of God in man. Wrong sentiments in regard to marriage had found a place in the minds of the teachers of Israel. They were making of none effect the sacred institution of marriage. Man was becoming so hardhearted that he would for the most trivial excuse separate from his wife, or, if he chose, he would separate her from the children and send her away. This was considered a great disgrace and was often accompanied by the most acute suffering on the part of the discarded one.

Christ came to correct these evils, and His first miracle was wrought on the occasion of the marriage. Thus He announced to the world that marriage when kept pure and undefiled is a sacred institution.

Counsel to One Contemplating Divorce: Your ideas in regard to the marriage relation have been erroneous. Nothing but the violation of the marriage bed can either break or annul the marriage vow. We are living in perilous times, when there is no assurance in anything save in firm, unwavering faith in Jesus Christ. There is no heart that may not be estranged from God through the devices of Satan, if one does not watch unto prayer.

Your health would have been in a far better condition had

your mind been at peace and rest; but it became confused and unbalanced, and you reasoned incorrectly in regard to the matter of divorce. Your views cannot be sustained on the ground from which you reason. Men are not at liberty to make a standard of law for themselves, to avoid God's law and please their own inclination. They must come to God's great moral standard of righteousness.

God gave only one cause why a wife should leave her husband, or the husband leave his wife, which was adultery. Let this ground be prayerfully considered.

To a Deserted Husband: I cannot see what more can be done in this case, and I think that the only thing that you can do is to give up your wife. If she is thus determined not to live with you, both she and you would be most miserable to attempt it. And as she has fully and determinedly set her stakes, you can only shoulder your cross and show yourself a man.

Still Married in God's Sight, Although Divorced: A woman may be legally divorced from her husband by the laws of the land and yet not divorced in the sight of God and according to the higher law. There is only one sin, which is adultery, which can place the husband or wife in a position where they can be free from the marriage vow in the sight of God. Although the laws of the land may grant a divorce, yet they are husband and wife still in the Bible light, according to the laws of God.

THE AGED PARENTS

"Honour Thy Father and Thy Mother": The obligation resting upon children to honor their parents is of lifelong duration. If the parents are feeble and old, the affection and attention of the children should be bestowed in proportion to the need of father and mother. Nobly, decidedly, the children should shape their course of action even if it requires self-denial, so that every thought of anxiety and perplexity may be removed from the minds of the parents.

Children should be educated to love and care tenderly for father and mother. Care for them, children, yourselves; for no other hand can do the little acts of kindness with the acceptance that you can do them. Improve your precious opportunity to scatter seeds of kindness.

Let children carefully remember that at the best the aged parents have but little joy and comfort. What can bring greater sorrow to their hearts than manifest neglect on the part of their children? What sin can be worse in children than to bring grief to an aged, helpless father or mother?

Smooth the Pathway: After children grow to years of maturity, some of them think their duty is done in providing an abode for their parents. While giving them food and shelter, they give them no love or sympathy. In their parents' old age, when they long for expression of affection and sympathy, children heartlessly deprive them of their attention. There is no time when children should withhold respect and love from their father and mother. While the parents live, it should be the children's joy to honor and respect them. They should bring all the cheerfulness and sunshine into the life of the aged parents that they possibly can. They should smooth their pathway to the grave. There is no better recommendation in this world than that a child has honored his parents, no better record in the books of heaven than that he has loved and honored father and mother.

Some Parents Are Responsible for Disrespect: When parents permit a child to show them disrespect in childhood, allowing them to speak pettishly and even harshly, there will be a dreadful harvest to be reaped in afteryears. When parents fail to require prompt and perfect obedience in their children, they fail to lay the right foundation of character in their little ones. They prepare their children to dishonor them when they are old, and bring sorrow to their hearts when they are nearing the grave, unless the grace of Christ changes the hearts and transforms the characters of their children.

If children think that they were treated with severity in their childhood, will it help them to grow in grace and in the knowledge of Christ, will it make them reflect His image, to cherish a spirit of retaliation and revenge against their parents, especially when they are old and feeble? Will not the very helplessness of the parents plead for the children's love? Will not the necessities of the aged father and mother call forth the noble feelings of the heart, and through the grace of Christ, shall not the parents be treated with kind attention and respect by their offspring? Oh, let not the heart be made as adamant as steel against father and mother!

Show No Retaliation: Said one of her mother, "I always hated my mother, and my mother hated me." These words stand registered in the books of heaven to be opened and revealed in the day of judgment when everyone shall be rewarded according to his works.

Be Patient With Infirmities: Especially dreadful is the thought of a child turning in hatred upon a mother who has become old and feeble, upon whom has come those infirmities of disposition attendant upon second childhood. How patiently, how tenderly, should children bear with such a mother! Tender words which will not irritate the spirit should be spoken. A true Christian will never be unkind, never under any circumstances be neglectful of his father or mother, but will heed the command, "Honour thy father and thy mother."

A Happy Privilege: The thought that children have ministered to the comfort of their parents is a thought of satisfaction all through the life, and will especially bring them joy when they themselves are in need of sympathy and love. Those whose hearts are filled with love will regard the privilege of smoothing the passage to the grave for their parents an inestimable privilege. They will rejoice that they had a part in bringing comfort and peace to the last days of their loved parents. To do otherwise than this, to deny to the helpless aged ones the kindly ministrations of sons and daughters, would fill the soul with remorse, the days with regret, if our hearts were not hardened and cold as a stone.

STEWARDS OF GOD

Recognize God's Ownership: That which lies at the foundation of business integrity and of true success is the recognition of God's ownership. The Creator of all things, He is the original proprietor. We are His stewards. All that we have is a trust from Him, to be used according to His direction.

This is an obligation that rests upon every human being. It has to do with the whole sphere of human activity. Whether we recognize it or not, we are stewards, supplied from God with talents and facilities and placed in the world to do a work appointed by Him.

Money is not ours; houses and grounds, pictures and furniture, garments and luxuries, do not belong to us. We are pilgrims, we are strangers. We have only a grant of those things that are necessary for health and life. Our temporal blessings are given us in trust, to prove whether we can be entrusted with eternal riches. If we endure the proving of God, then we shall receive that purchased possession which is to be our own—glory, honor, and immortality.

We Must Give an Account: We should ever remember that in the judgment we must meet the record of the way we use God's money. Much is spent in self-pleasing, self-gratification, that does us no real good, but positive injury. If we realize that God is the giver of all good things, that the money is His, then we shall exercise wisdom in its expenditure, conforming to His holy will.

Make God's Requirements First: God's requirements come first. We are not doing His will if we consecrate to Him what is left of our income after all our imaginary wants have been supplied. Before any part of our earnings is consumed, we should take out and present to Him that portion which He claims. If we have prosperity in our secular business, it is because God blesses us. A part of this income is to be devoted to the poor, and a large portion to be applied to the cause of God. When that which God claims is rendered to Him, the remainder will be sanctified and blessed to our own use. But when a man robs God by withholding that which He requires, His curse rests upon the whole.

Remember the Poor: If we represent the character of Christ, every particle of selfishness must be expelled from the soul. In carrying forward the work He gave to our hands, it will be necessary for us to give every jot and tittle of our means that we can spare. Poverty and distress in families will come to our knowledge, and afflicted and suffering ones will have to be relieved. We know very little of the human suffering that exists everywhere about us; but as we have opportunity, we should be ready to render immediate assistance to those who are under a severe pressure.

PRINCIPLES OF FAMILY FINANCE

A Blessing or a Curse: Money is not necessarily a curse; it is of high value because if rightly appropriated, it can do good in the salvation of souls, in blessing others who are poorer than ourselves. By an improvident or unwise use, money will become a snare to the user. He who employs money to gratify pride and ambition makes it a curse rather than a blessing. Money is a constant test of the affections. Whoever acquires more than sufficient for his real needs should seek wisdom and grace to know his own heart and to keep his heart diligently, lest he have imaginary wants and become an unfaithful steward, using with prodigality his Lord's entrusted capital.

Security in Home Ownership: If the laws given by God had continued to be carried out, how different would be the present condition of the world, morally, spiritually, and temporally. Selfishness and self-importance would not be manifested as now, but each would cherish a kind regard for the happiness and welfare of others. Instead of the poorer classes being kept under the iron heel of oppression by the wealthy, instead of having other men's brains to think and plan for them in temporal as well as in spiritual things, they would have some chance for independence of thought and action.

The sense of being owners of their own homes would inspire them with a strong desire for improvement. They would soon acquire skill in planning and devising for themselves; their children would be educated to habits of industry and economy, and the intellect would be greatly strengthened. They would feel that they are men, not slaves, and would be able to regain to a great degree their lost self-respect and moral independence.

A Praiseworthy Independence: Independence of one kind is praiseworthy. To desire to bear your own weight and not to eat the bread of dependence is right. It is a noble, generous ambition that dictates the wish to be self-supporting. Industrious habits and frugality are necessary.

Balancing the Budget: Many, very many, have not so educated themselves that they can keep their expenditures within the limit of their income. They do not learn to adapt themselves to circumstances, and they borrow and borrow again and again and become overwhelmed in debt, and consequently they become discouraged and disheartened.

Keep a Record of Expenditures: Habits of self-indulgence or a want of tact and skill on the part of the wife and mother may be a constant drain upon the treasury; and yet that mother may think she is doing her best because she has never been taught to restrict her wants or the wants of her children and has never acquired skill and tact in household matters. Hence one family may require for its support twice the amount that would suffice for another family of the same size.

All should learn how to keep accounts. Some neglect this work as nonessential, but this is wrong. All expenses should be accurately stated.

Indulgence Is Not Love: Do not educate your children to think that your love for them must be expressed by indulgence of their pride, extravagance, and love of display. There is no time now to invent ways for using up money. Use your inventive faculties in seeking to economize.

Unwise Economy: God is not honored when the body is neglected or abused and is thus unfitted for His service. To care for the body by providing for it food that is relishable and strengthening is one of the first duties of the householder. It is far better to have less expensive clothing and furniture than to stint the supply of food.

Some householders stint the family table in order to provide expensive entertainment for visitors. This is unwise. In the entertainment of guests there should be greater simplicity. Let the needs of the family have first attention.

Unwise economy and artificial customs often prevent the exercise of hospitality where it is needed and would be a blessing. The regular supply of food for our tables should be such that the unexpected guest can be made welcome without burdening the housewife to make extra preparation.

Wife's Allowance for Personal Use: You should allow your wife a certain sum weekly and should let her do what she pleases with this money. You have not given her opportunity to exercise her tact or her taste because you have not a proper realization of the position that a wife should occupy. Your wife has an excellent and a well-balanced mind.

We cannot make the heart purer or holier by clothing the body in sackcloth or depriving the home of all that ministers to comfort, taste, or convenience.

God does not require that His people should deprive themselves of that which is really necessary for their health and comfort, but He does not approve of wantonness and extravagance and display.

When to Spare and When to Spend: You should learn to know when to spare and when to spend. We cannot be Christ's followers unless we deny self and lift the cross. We should pay up squarely as we go; gather up the dropped stitches; bind off your raveling edges, and know just what you can call your own. You should reckon up all the littles spent in self-gratification.

You should notice what is used simply to gratify taste and in cultivating a perverted, epicurian appetite. The money expended for useless delicacies might be used to add to your substantial home comforts and conveniences. You are not to be penurious; you are to be honest with yourself and your brethren. Penuriousness is an abuse of God's bounties. Lavishness is also an abuse. The little outgoes that you think of as not worth mentioning amount to considerable in the end.

You Will Know: It is not necessary to specify here how economy may be practiced in every particular. Those whose hearts are fully surrendered to God, and who take His Word as their guide, will know how to conduct themselves in all the duties of life. They will learn of Jesus, who is meek and lowly of heart; and in cultivating the meekness of Christ, they will close the door against innumerable temptations.

PRACTICING  ECONOMY

How Christ Taught Economy: Christ once gave His disciples a lesson upon economy which is worthy of careful attention. He wrought a miracle to feed the hungry thousands who had listened to His teaching; yet after all had eaten and were satisfied, He did not permit the fragments to be wasted. He who could, in their necessity, feed the vast multitude by His divine power bade His disciples gather up the fragments, that nothing might be lost. This lesson was given as much for our benefit as for those living in Christ's day. The Son of God has a care for the necessities of temporal life. He did not neglect the broken fragments after the feast, although He could make such a feast whenever He chose.

Follow His Self-denial: In order to become acquainted with the disappointments and trials and griefs that come to human beings, Christ reached to the lowest depths of woe and humiliation. He has traveled the path that He asks His followers to travel. He says to them, "If any man will come after me, let him deny himself, and take up his cross daily, and follow me." But professing Christians are not always willing to practice the self-denial that the Saviour calls for. They are not willing to bind about their wishes and desires in order that they may have more to give to the Lord. One says, "My family are expensive in their tastes, and it costs much to keep them." This shows that he and they need to learn the lessons of economy taught by the life of Christ.

To all comes the temptation to gratify selfish, extravagant desires, but let us remember that the Lord of life and glory came to this world to teach humanity the lesson of self-denial.

Those who do not live for self will not use up every dollar meeting their supposed wants and supplying their conveniences, but will bear in mind that they are Christ's followers, and that there are others who are in need of food and clothing.

Why Economize: Much might be said to the young people regarding their privilege to help the cause of God by learning lessons of economy and self-denial. Many think that they must indulge in this pleasure and that, and in order to do this, they accustom themselves to live up to the full extent of their income. God wants us to do better in this respect.

We sin against ourselves when we are satisfied with enough to eat and drink and wear. God has something higher than this

143

before us. When we are willing to put away our selfish desires and give the powers of heart and mind to the work of the cause of God, heavenly agencies will cooperate with us, making us a blessing to humanity.

Even though he may be poor, the youth who is industrious and economical can save a little for the cause of God.

Watch the Pennies and Nickels: Waste not your pennies in purchasing unnecessary things. You may think these little sums do not amount to much, but these many littles will prove a great whole. If we could, we would plead for the means that is spent in needless things, in dress and selfish indulgence. Poverty in every shape is on every hand. And God has made it our duty to relieve suffering humanity in every way possible.

The Lord would have His people thoughtful and caretaking. He would have them study economy in everything, and waste nothing.

The amount daily spent in needless things, with the thought, "It is only a nickel," "It is only a dime," seems very little; but multiply these littles by the days of the year, and as the years go by, the array of figures will seem almost incredible.

Practice Economy From Principle: Those whose hands are open to respond to the calls for means to sustain the cause of God and to relieve the suffering and the needy are not the ones who are found loose and lax and dilatory in their business management. They are always careful to keep their outgoes within their income. They are economical from principle; they feel it their duty to save, that they may have something to give.

INSTRUCTING CHILDREN ABOUT MONEY

Teach Simple Habits Every Day: Parents are to bring up and educate and train their children in habits of self-control and self-denial. They are ever to keep before them their obligation to obey the Word of God and to live for the purpose of serving Jesus. They are to educate their children that there is need of living in accordance with simple habits in their daily life, and to avoid expensive dress, expensive diet, expensive houses, and expensive furniture.

When very young, children should be educated to read, to write, to understand figures, to keep their own accounts. They may go forward, advancing step by step in this knowledge. But before everything else, they should be taught that the fear of the Lord is the beginning of wisdom.

Youth to Be Considerate: Through erroneous ideas regarding the use of money the youth are exposed to many dangers. They are not to be carried along and supplied with money as if there were an inexhaustible supply from which they could draw to gratify every supposed need. Money is to be regarded as a gift entrusted to us of God to do His work, to build up His kingdom, and the youth should learn to restrict their desires.

Give Lessons in Money Values: Money which comes to the young with but little effort on their part will not be valued. Some have to obtain money by hard work and privation, but how much safer are those youth who know just where their spending money comes from, who know what their clothing and food costs, and what it takes to purchase a home!

There are many ways in which children can earn money themselves and can act their part in bringing thank offerings to Jesus, who gave His own life for them. They should be taught that the money which they earn is not theirs to spend as their inexperienced minds may choose, but to use judiciously and to give to missionary purposes. They should not be satisfied to take money from their father or mother and put it into the treasury as an offering, when it is not theirs. They should say to themselves, "Shall I give of that which costs me nothing?"

The children may learn to show their love for Christ by denying themselves needless trifles, for the purchase of which much money slips through their fingers. In every family this work should be done. It requires tact and method, but it will be the best education the children can receive. And if all the little children would present their offerings to the Lord, their gifts would be as little rivulets which, when united and set flowing, would swell into a river.

Parents' Best Legacy to Children: The very best legacy which parents can leave their children is a knowledge of useful labor and the example of a life characterized by disinterested benevolence. By such a life they show the true value of money, that it is only to be appreciated for the good that it will accomplish in relieving their own wants and the necessities of others, and in advancing the cause of God.

BUSINESS INTEGRITY

Source Book of Business Principles: There is no branch of legitimate business for which the Bible does not afford an essential preparation. Its principles of diligence, honesty, thrift, temperance, and purity are the secret of true success. These principles, as set forth in the Book of Proverbs, constitute a treasury of practical wisdom. Where can the merchant, the artisan, the director of men in any department of business, find better maxims for himself or for his employees than are found in these words of the wise man:

"Seest thou a man diligent in his business? He shall stand before kings; he shall not stand before mean men."

"In all labour there is profit: but the talk of the lips tendeth only to penury."

"The soul of the sluggard desireth, and hath nothing."

"The drunkard and the glutton shall come to poverty· and drowsiness shall clothe a man with rags."

How many a man might have escaped financial failure and ruin by heeding the warnings so often repeated and emphasized in the Scriptures:

"He that maketh haste to be rich shall not be innocent."

"Wealth gotten in haste shall be diminished; but he that gathereth by labour shall have increase."

147

"The getting of treasures by a lying tongue is a vanity tossed to and fro of them that seek death."

"The borrower is servant to the lender."

"He that is surety for a stranger shall smart for it: and he that hateth suretiship is sure."

As we deal with our fellowmen in petty dishonesty or in more daring fraud, so will we deal with God. Men who persist in a course of dishonesty will carry out their principles until they cheat their own souls and lose heaven and eternal life. They will sacrifice honor and religion for a small worldly advantage.

Counsel to One in Debt: Be determined never to incur another debt. Deny yourself a thousand things rather than run in debt. This has been the curse of your life, getting into debt. Avoid it as you would the smallpox.

Make a solemn covenant with God that by His blessing you will pay your debts and then owe no man anything if you live on porridge and bread. It is so easy in preparing your table to throw out of your pocket twenty-five cents for extras. Take care of the pennies, and the dollars will take care of themselves. It is the mites here and the mites there that are spent for this, that, and the other that soon run up into dollars. Deny self at least while you are walled in with debts. Do not falter, be discouraged, or turn back. Deny your taste, deny the indulgence of appetite, save your pence, and pay your debts. Work them off as fast as possible. When you can stand forth a free man again, owing no man anything, you will have achieved a great victory.

Danger in Extreme Positions: Some are not discreet and would incur debts that might be avoided. Others exercise a caution that savors of unbelief. By taking advantage of circumstances we may at times invest means to such advantage that the work of God will be strengthened and upbuilt, and yet keep strictly to right principles.

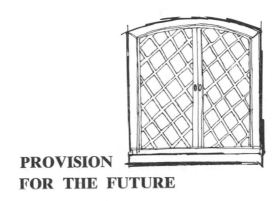

PROVISION
FOR THE FUTURE

This Counsel May Help You: You have been in a business which would at times yield you large profits at once. After you have earned means, you have not studied to economize in reference to a time when means could not be earned so easily, but have expended much for imaginary wants. Had you and your wife understood it to be a duty that God enjoined upon you to deny your taste and your desires and make provision for the future instead of living merely for the present, you could now have had a competency and your family have had the comforts of life. You have a lesson to learn. It is to make a little go the longest way.

Save Systematically: You might today have had a capital of means to use in case of emergency and to aid the cause of God, if you had economized as you should. Every week a portion of your wages should be reserved and in no case touched unless suffering actual want, or to render back to the Giver in offerings to God.

The means you have earned has not been wisely and economically expended so as to leave a margin should you be sick and your family deprived of the means you bring to sustain them. Your family should have something to rely upon if you should be brought into straitened places.

Advice Concerning a Savings Account: Every week you should lay by in some secure place five or ten dollars not to be used up unless in case of sickness. With economy you may place something at interest. With wise management you can save something after paying your debts.

Remember God's Cause: Let no one think that he will meet the mind of Christ in hoarding up property through life and then at death making a bequest of a portion of it to some benevolent cause.

Make a Will: Many are not exercised upon the subject of making their wills while they are in apparent health. But this precaution should be taken. They should know their financial standing and should not allow their business to become entangled. They should arrange their property in such a manner that they may leave it at any time.

Wills should be made in a manner to stand the test of the law. After they are drawn, they may remain for years and do no harm.

The Curse of Hoarded Wealth: Those who acquire wealth for the purpose of hoarding it leave the curse of wealth to their children. It is a sin, an awful, soul-periling sin for fathers and mothers to do this, and this sin extends to their posterity. Often the children spend their means in foolish extravagance, in riotous living, so that they become beggars. They know not the value of the inheritance they have squandered. Had their fathers and mothers set them a proper example, not in hoarding but in imparting their wealth, they would have laid up for themselves treasure in heaven and received a return even in this world of peace and happiness and in the future life eternal riches.

PORTALS WE MUST WATCH

Demoralizing Influences All About Us: There is reason for deep solicitude on your part for your children, who have temptations to encounter at every advance step. It is impossible for them to avoid contact with evil associates. They will see sights, hear sounds, and be subjected to influences which are demoralizing and which, unless they are thoroughly guarded, will imperceptibly but surely corrupt the heart and deform the character.

Avoid Reading, Seeing, or Hearing Evil: The Apostle Peter sought to teach the believers how important it is to keep the mind from wandering to forbidden themes or from spending its energies on trifling subjects. Those who would not fall a prey to Satan's devices must guard well the avenues of the soul; they must avoid reading, seeing, or hearing that which will suggest impure thoughts. The mind must not be left to dwell at random upon every subject that the enemy of souls may suggest. The heart must be faithfully sentineled, or evils without will awaken evils within, and the soul will wander in darkness.

Guard the Eyes and Ears: Everything that can be done should be done to place ourselves and our children where we shall not see the iniquity that is practiced in the world. We should carefully guard the sight of our eyes and the hearing of our ears so that these awful things shall not enter our minds.

A Bulwark Against Temptation: In Christian homes a bulwark should be built against temptation. Satan is using every means to make crime and degrading vice popular. The mind is educated to familiarity with sin. The course pursued by the base and vile is kept before the people in the periodicals of the day, and everything that can arouse passion is brought before them.

Sow Lawlessness, Reap Crime: Many of the popular publications of the day are filled with sensational stories that are educating the youth in wickedness and leading them in the path to perdition. Mere children in years are old in a knowledge of crime. They are incited to evil by the tales they read. In imagination they act over the deeds portrayed, until their ambition is aroused to see what they can do in committing crime and evading punishment.

To the active minds of children and youth the scenes pictured in imaginary revelations of the future are realities. As revolutions are predicted and all manner of proceedings described that break down the barriers of law and self-restraint, many catch the spirit of these representations. They are led to the commission of crimes even worse, if possible, than these sensational writers depict. Through such influences as these society is becoming demoralized. The seeds of lawlessness are sown broadcast. None need marvel that a harvest of crime is the result.

I Will See No Wicked Thing: Parents must exercise unceasing watchfulness that their children be not lost to God. The vows of David, recorded in the 101st Psalm, should be the vows of all upon whom rest the responsibilities of guarding the influences of the home. The psalmist declares, "I will set no wicked thing before mine eyes."

Say firmly, "I will not spend precious moments in reading that which will be of no profit to me. I will close my eyes to frivolous and sinful things. My ears are the Lord's, and I will not listen to the subtle reasoning of the enemy. My voice shall not in any way be subject to a will that is not under the influence of the Spirit of God. My body is the temple of the Holy Spirit, and every power of my being shall be consecrated to worthy pursuits."

Feed the Child's Mind With Proper Food: The susceptible, expanding mind of the child longs for knowledge. Parents should keep themselves well informed, that they may give the minds of their children proper food. Like the body, the mind derives its strength from the food it receives. It is broadened and elevated by pure, strengthening thoughts; but it is narrowed and debased by thoughts that are of the earth earthy.

Parents, you are the ones to decide whether the minds of your children shall be filled with ennobling thoughts or with vicious sentiments. You cannot keep their active minds unoccupied; neither can you frown away evil. Only by the inculcation of right principles can you exclude wrong thoughts. Unless parents plant the seeds of truth in the hearts of their children, the enemy will sow tares. Good, sound instruction is the only preventive of the evil communications that corrupt good manners. Truth will protect the soul from the endless temptations that must be encountered.

Parents to Control Reading Habits: Many youth are eager for books. They read anything that they can obtain. I appeal to the parents of such children to control their desire for reading. Encourage your children to store the mind with valuable knowledge, to let that which is good occupy the soul and control its powers, leaving no place for low, debasing thoughts. Restrict the desire for reading matter that does not furnish good food for the mind.

Children need proper reading which will afford amusement and recreation and not demoralize the mind or weary the body. If they are taught to love romance and newspaper tales, instructive books and papers will become distasteful to them. Most children and young people will have reading matter; and if it is not selected for them, they will select it for themselves. They can find a ruinous quality of reading anywhere, and they soon learn to love it; but if pure and good reading is furnished them, they will cultivate a taste for that.

Discipline and Educate Mental Tastes: The mental tastes must be disciplined and educated with the greatest care. Parents must begin early to unfold the Scriptures to the expanding minds of their children, that proper habits of thought may be formed.

No effort should be spared to establish right habits of study. If the mind wanders, bring it back. If the intellectual and moral tastes have been perverted by overwrought and exciting tales of fiction so that there is a disinclination to apply the mind, there is a battle to be fought to overcome this habit. A love for fictitious reading should be overcome at once. Rigid rules should be enforced to hold the mind in the proper channel.

Prevalence of Harmful Books: The world is deluged with books that might better be consumed than circulated. Books on sensational topics, published and circulated as a money-making scheme, might better never be read by the youth. There is a satanic fascination in such books.

Non-Christian Authors: Another source of danger against which we should be constantly on guard is the reading of infidel authors. Such works are inspired by the enemy of truth, and no one can read them without imperiling the soul. It is true that some who are affected by them may finally recover; but all who tamper with their evil influence place themselves on Satan's ground, and he makes the most of his advantage. As they invite his temptations, they have not wisdom to discern or strength to resist them. With a fascinating, bewitching power unbelief and infidelity fasten themselves upon the mind.

Never should books containing a perversion of truth be placed in the hands of children or youth. Let not our children, in the very process of obtaining an education, receive ideas that will prove to be seeds of sin.

Hasty, Superficial Reading: With the immense tide of printed matter constantly pouring from the press, old and young form the habit of reading hastily and superficially, and the mind loses its power of connected and vigorous thought. Furthermore, a large share of the periodicals and books that, like the frogs of Egypt, are overspreading the land are not merely commonplace, idle, and enervating, but unclean and degrading. Their effect is not merely to intoxicate and ruin the mind, but to corrupt and destroy the soul.

How Mental Vigor Is Destroyed: There are few well-balanced minds because parents are wickedly negligent of their duty to stimulate weak traits and repress wrong ones. They do not remember that they are under the most solemn obligation to watch the tendencies of each child, that it is their duty to train their children to right habits and right ways of thinking.

Cultivate the moral and intellectual powers. Let not these noble powers become enfeebled and perverted by much reading of even storybooks. I know of strong minds that have been unbalanced and partially benumbed, or paralyzed, by intemperance in reading.

The Untrained Mind: Between an uncultivated field and an untrained mind there is a striking similarity. In the minds of children and youth the enemy sows tares, and unless parents keep watchful guard, these will spring up to bear their evil fruit. Unceasing care is needed in cultivating the soil of the mind and sowing it with the precious seed of Bible truth.

Children should be taught to reject trashy, exciting tales and to turn to sensible reading, which will lead the mind to take an interest in Bible story, history, and argument. Reading that will throw light upon the Sacred Volume and quicken the desire to study it is not dangerous, but beneficial.

It is impossible for the youth to possess a healthy tone of mind and correct religious principles unless they enjoy the perusal of the Word of God. This Book contains the most interesting history, points out the way of salvation through Christ, and is their guide to a higher and better life.

COURTESY AND KINDNESS

Courtesy Will Banish Half Life's Ills: The principle inculcated by the injunction, "Be kindly affectioned one to another," lies at the very foundation of domestic happiness. Christian courtesy should reign in every household. It is cheap, but it has power to soften natures which would grow hard and rough without it. The cultivation of a uniform courtesy, a willingness

157

to do by others as we would like them to do by us, would banish half the ills of life.

It Begins at Home: If we would have our children practice kindness, courtesy, and love, we ourselves must set them the example.

Courtesy, even in little things, should be manifested by the parents toward each other. Universal kindness should be the law of the house. No rude language should be indulged; no bitter words should be spoken.

All may possess a cheerful countenance, a gentle voice, a courteous manner; and these are elements of power. Children are attracted by a cheerful, sunny demeanor. Show them kindness and courtesy, and they will manifest the same spirit toward you and toward one another.

Mutual Kindness: By speaking kindly to their children and praising them when they try to do right, parents may encourage their efforts, make them very happy, and throw around the family circle a charm which will chase away every dark shadow and bring cheerful sunlight in. Mutual kindness and forbearance will make home a Paradise and attract holy angels into the family circle; but they will flee from a house where there are unpleasant words, fretfulness, and strife. Unkindness, complaining, and anger shut Jesus from the dwelling.

The essence of true politeness is consideration for others. The essential, enduring education is that which broadens the sympathies and encourages universal kindliness. That so-called culture which does not make a youth deferential toward his parents, appreciative of their excellences, forbearing toward their defects, and helpful to their necessities; which does not make him considerate and tender, generous and helpful toward the young, the old, and the unfortunate, and courteous toward all is a failure.

The Golden Rule is the principle of true courtesy, and its truest illustration is seen in the life and character of Jesus. Oh, what rays of softness and beauty shone forth in the daily life of our Saviour! What sweetness flowed from His very presence! The same spirit will be revealed in His children. Those with whom Christ dwells will be surrounded with a divine atmosphere.

The Best Treatise on Etiquette: The most valuable treatise on etiquette ever penned is the precious instruction given by the Saviour, with the utterance of the Holy Spirit through the Apostle Paul—words that should be ineffaceably written in the memory of every human being, young or old:

"As I have loved you, that ye also love one another."

> "Love suffereth long, and is kind;
>   Love envieth not;
>   Love vaunteth not itself,
>   Is not puffed up,
> Doth not behave itself unseemly,
>   Seeketh not its own,
>   Is not provoked,
>   Taketh not account of evil;
> Rejoiceth not in unrighteousness,
> But rejoiceth with the truth;
> Beareth all things, believeth all things,
> Hopeth all things, endureth all things.
>   Love never faileth."

Love Motivates True Courtesy: The most careful cultivation of the outward proprieties of life is not sufficient to shut out all fretfulness, harsh judgment, and unbecoming speech. True refinement will never be revealed so long as self is considered as the supreme object. Love must dwell in the heart. A thoroughgoing Christian draws his motives of action from his deep heart-love for his Master. Up through the roots of his affection for Christ springs an unselfish interest in his brethren.

True courtesy is not learned by the mere practice of rules of etiquette. Propriety of deportment is at all times to be observed; wherever principle is not compromised, consideration of others will lead to compliance with accepted customs; but true courtesy requires no sacrifice of principle to conventionality. It ignores caste. It teaches self-respect, respect for the dignity of man as man, a regard for every member of the great human brotherhood.

Gentle manners, cheerful conversation, and loving acts will bind the hearts of children to their parents by the silken cords of affection and will do more to make home attractive than the rarest ornaments that can be bought for gold.

Varied Temperaments Must Blend: It is in the order of God that persons of varied temperament should associate together. When this is the case, each member of the household should sacredly regard the feelings and respect the rights of the others. By this means mutual consideration and forbearance will be cultivated, prejudices will be softened, and rough points of character smoothed. Harmony may be secured, and the blending of the varied temperaments may be a benefit to each.

Nothing Will Atone for Lack of Courtesy: Those who profess to be followers of Christ and are at the same time rough, unkind, and uncourteous in words and deportment have not learned of Jesus. A blustering, overbearing, faultfinding man is not a Christian; for to be a Christian is to be Christlike. The conduct of some professed Christians is so lacking in kindness and courtesy that their good is evil spoken of. Their sincerity may not be doubted; their uprightness may not be questioned, but sincerity and uprightness will not atone for a lack of kindness and courtesy. The Christian is to be sympathetic as well as true, pitiful and courteous as well as upright and honest.

True Courtesy Lights the World: If we are courteous and gentle at home, we shall carry the savor of a pleasant disposition when away from home. If we manifest forbearance, patience, meekness, and fortitude in the home, we shall be able to be a light to the world.

CHEERFULNESS

Life Is What We Make It: Do not allow the perplexities and worries of everyday life to fret your mind and cloud your brow. If you do, you will always have something to vex and annoy. Life is what we make it, and we shall find what we look for. If we look for sadness and trouble, if we are in a frame of mind to magnify little difficulties, we shall find plenty of them to engross our thoughts and our conversation. But if we look on the bright side of things, we shall find enough to make us cheerful and happy. If we give smiles, they will be returned to us; if we speak pleasant, cheerful words, they will be spoken to us again.

When Christians appear as gloomy and depressed as though they thought themselves friendless, they give a wrong impression of religion. In some cases the idea has been entertained that cheerfulness is inconsistent with the dignity of the Christian character, but this is a mistake. Heaven is all joy; and if we gather to our souls the joys of heaven and, as far as possible, express them in our words and deportment, we shall be more pleasing to our heavenly Father than if we were gloomy and sad.

Winning the Affection of Children: Smile, parents; smile, teachers. If your heart is sad, let not your face reveal the fact. Let the sunshine from a loving, grateful heart light up the countenance. Unbend from your iron dignity, adapt yourselves to the children's needs, and make them love you. You must win their affection, if you would impress religious truth upon their heart.

Keep a Pleasant Countenance: Parents, be cheerful, not common and cheap, but be thankful and obedient and submissive to your heavenly Father. You are not at liberty to act out your feelings if things should arise that irritate. Winning love is to be like deep waters, ever flowing forth in the management of your children. They are the lambs of the flock of God. Bring your little ones to Christ. If parents would educate their children to be pleasant, they should never speak in a scolding manner to them. Educate yourself to carry a pleasant countenance, and bring all the sweetness and melody possible into your voice. The angels of God are ever near your little ones, and your harsh loud tones of fretfulness are not pleasant to their ears.

Lift the Shadows and Lighten the Task: Look upon matters in a cheerful light, seeking to lift the shadows that, if cherished, will envelop the soul. Cultivate sympathy for others. Let cheerfulness, kindness, and love pervade the home. This will increase a love for religious exercises, and duties large and small will be performed with a light heart.

SPEECH

The Voice Is a Talent: The voice is an entrusted talent, and it should be used to help and encourage and strengthen our fellowmen. If parents will love God and keep the way of the Lord to do justice and judgment, their language will not savor of sickly sentimentalism. It will be of a sound, pure, edifying character. Whether they are at home or abroad, their words will be well chosen. They will descend to no cheapness.

Angels hear the words that are spoken in the home. Therefore, never scold; but let the influence of your words be such that it will ascend to heaven as fragrant incense.

Parents should keep the atmosphere of the home pure and fragrant with kind words, with tender sympathy and love; but at the same time they are to be firm and unyielding in principle. If you are firm with your children, they may think that you do not love them. This you may expect, but never manifest harshness. Justice and mercy must clasp hands; there must be no wavering or impulsive movements.

An Outward Expression of Inward Grace: The chief requisite of language is that it be pure and kind and true—"the outward expression of an inward grace." The best school for this language study is the home.

Be pure in speech. Cultivate a soft and persuasive, not a harsh and dictatorial, tone of voice. Give the children lessons in voice culture. Train their habits of speech, until no coarse or rough words will come spontaneously from their lips when any trial comes to them.

Harsh, Scolding Words: In a home where harsh, fretful, scolding words are spoken, a child cries much; and upon its tender sensibilities are impressed the marks of unhappiness and discord. Then, mothers, let your countenance be full of sunshine. Smile, if you can, and the infant's mind and heart will reflect the light of your countenance as the polished plate of an artist portrays the human features. Be sure, mothers, to have an indwelling Christ so that on your child's plastic mind may be impressed the divine likeness.

No Jarring Note: Allow nothing like strife or dissension to come into the home. Speak gently. Never raise your voice to harshness. Keep yourselves calm. Put away faultfinding and all untruthfulness. Tell the children that you want to help them to prepare for a holy heaven, where all is peace, where not one jarring note is heard. Be patient with them in their trials, which may look small to you but which are large to them.

Sunshine or Shadow? It is important that children and youth should be trained to guard their words and deeds; for their course of action causes sunshine or shadow, not only in their own home, but also with all with whom they come in contact.

Let only pleasant words be spoken by parents to their children, and respectful words by children to their parents.

Angry, Hasty Words: When you speak angry words to your children, you are helping the cause of the enemy of all righteousness. Let every child have a fair chance from babyhood up. The work of teaching should begin in childhood, not accompanied by harshness and fretting, but in kindness and patience; and this instruction should be continued through all their years to manhood and womanhood.

What harm is wrought in the family circle by the utterance of impatient words, for the impatient utterance of one leads another to retort in the same spirit and manner. Then come words of retaliation, words of self-justification, and it is by such words that a heavy, galling yoke is manufactured for your neck; for all these bitter words will come back in a baleful harvest to your soul.

A Pledge Suggested: It would be well for every man to sign a pledge to speak kindly in his home, to let the law of love rule his speech. Parents, never speak hastily. If your children do wrong, correct them, but let your words be full of tenderness and love. Every time you scold, you lose a precious opportunity of giving a lesson in forbearance and patience. Let love be the most prominent feature in your correction of wrong.

Table Conversation: How many families season their daily meals with doubt and questionings! They dissect the characters of their friends and serve them up as a dainty dessert. A precious bit of slander is passed around the board to be commented upon, not only by adults, but by children. In this God is dishonored.

Let the conversation at the family board be such as is calculated to leave a fragrant influence on the minds of the children.

Fathers and mothers, speak kindly to your children; remember how sensitive you are, how little you can bear to be blamed; reflect, and know that your children are like you. That which you cannot bear do not lay upon them. If you cannot bear censure and blame, neither can your children, who are weaker than you and cannot endure as much. Let your pleasant, cheerful words ever be like sunbeams in your family. The fruits of self-control, thoughtfulness, and painstaking on your part will be a hundredfold.

HOSPITALITY

Neglected Opportunities and Privileges: "A lover of hospitality" is among the specifications given by the Holy Spirit as marking one who is to bear responsibility in the church. And to the whole church is given the injunction: "Use hospitality one to another without grudging. As every man hath received the gift, even so minister the same one to another, as good stewards of the manifold grace of God."

166

These admonitions have been strangely neglected. Even among those who profess to be Christians true hospitality is little exercised.

Blessings Lost by Selfish Exclusiveness: God is displeased with the selfish interest so often manifested for "me and my family." Every family that cherishes this spirit needs to be converted by the pure principles exemplified in the life of Christ. Those who shut themselves up within themselves, who are unwilling to be drawn upon to entertain visitors, lose many blessings.

"When thou makest a dinner or a supper," Christ says, "call not thy friends, nor thy brethren, neither thy kinsmen, nor thy rich neighbours; lest they also bid thee again, and a recompence be made thee. But when thou makest a feast, call the poor, the maimed, the lame, the blind: and thou shalt be blessed; for they cannot recompense thee: for thou shalt be recompensed at the resurrection of the just."

These are guests whom it will lay on you no great burden to receive. You will not need to provide for them elaborate or expensive entertainment. You will need to make no effort at display. The warmth of a genial welcome, a place at your fireside, a seat at your home table, the privilege of sharing the blessing of the hour of prayer, would to many of these be like a glimpse of heaven.

Our sympathies are to overflow the boundaries of self and the enclosure of family walls. There are precious opportunities for those who will make their homes a blessing to others. Social influence is a wonderful power. We can use it, if we will, as a means of helping those about us.

A Refuge for Tempted Youth: Our homes should be a place of refuge for the tempted youth. Many there are who stand at the parting of the ways. Every influence, every impression, is determining the choice that shapes their destiny both here and hereafter. Evil invites them. Its resorts are made bright and attractive. They have a welcome for every comer. All about us are youth who have no home and many whose homes have no helpful, uplifting power, and the youth drift into evil. They are going down to ruin within the very shadow of our own doors.

These youth need a hand stretched out to them in sympathy. Kind words simply spoken, little attentions simply bestowed, will sweep away the clouds of temptations which gather over the soul. The true expression of heaven-born sympathy has power to open the door of hearts that need the fragrance of Christlike words and the simple, delicate touch of the spirit of Christ's love. If we would show an interest in the youth, invite them to our homes, and surround them with cheering, helpful influences, there are many who would gladly turn their steps into the upward path.

While you should treat your visitors kindly and make them feel at home, you should ever remember that you are a teacher to the little ones God has given you. They are watching you, and no course of yours should direct their feet in the wrong way. Be to your visitors just what you are to your family every day—pleasant, considerate, and courteous. In this way all can be educators, an example of good works. They testify that there is something more essential than to keep the mind on what they shall eat and drink and wherewithal they shall be clothed.

A Heavenly Expense Account: Christ keeps an account of every expense incurred in entertaining for His sake. He supplies all that is necessary for this work. Those who for Christ's sake entertain their brethren, doing their best to make the visit profitable both to their guests and to themselves, are recorded in heaven as worthy of special blessings.

YOUR

SOCIAL
NEEDS

The Influence of Friends: Everyone will find companions or make them. And just in proportion to the strength of the friendship will be the amount of influence which friends will exert over one another for good or for evil. All will have associates and will influence and be influenced in their turn.

God's Word places great stress upon the influence of association, even on men and women. How much greater is its power on the developing mind and character of children and youth! The company they keep, the principles they adopt, the habits they form, will decide the question of their usefulness here and of their future destiny.

It is inevitable that the youth will have associates, and they will necessarily feel their influence. There are mysterious links that bind souls together so that the heart of one answers to the heart of another. One catches the ideas, the sentiments, the spirit, of another. This association may be a blessing or a curse. The youth may help and strengthen one another, improving in deportment, in disposition, in knowledge; or, by permitting themselves to become careless and unfaithful, they may exert an influence that is demoralizing.

The Author of all beauty, Himself a lover of the beautiful, God provided to gratify in His children the love of beauty. He made provision also for their social needs, for the kindly and helpful associations that do so much to cultivate sympathy and to brighten and sweeten life.

Beware of Natural Tendencies: If the youth could be persuaded to associate with the pure, the thoughtful, and the amiable, the effect would be most salutary. If choice is made of companions who fear the Lord, the influence will lead to truth, to duty, and to holiness. A truly Christian life is a power for good. But, on the other hand, those who associate with men and women of questionable morals, of bad principles and practices, will soon be walking in the same path. The tendencies of the natural heart are downward. He who associates with the skeptic will soon become skeptical; he who chooses the companionship of the vile will most assuredly become vile. To walk in the counsel of the ungodly is the first step toward standing in the way of sinners and sitting in the seat of the scornful.

GUIDANCE IN
SOCIAL AFFAIRS

Bad Influences Almost Overpowering: The evil influence around our children is almost overpowering; it is corrupting their minds and leading them down to perdition. The minds of youth are naturally given to folly; and at an early age, before their characters are formed and their judgment matured, they frequently manifest a preference for associates who will have an injurious influence over them.

Could my voice reach the parents all through the land, I would warn them not to yield to the desires of their children in choosing their companions or associates. Little do parents consider that injurious impressions are far more readily received by the young than are divine impressions; therefore their associations should be the most favorable for the growth of grace and for the truth revealed in the Word of God to be established in the heart.

Let the youth be placed in the most favorable circumstances possible; for the company they keep, the principles they adopt, the habits they form, will settle the question of their usefulness here and of their future, eternal interests with a certainty that is infallible.

The Peril of Unlimited Freedom: Parents, your sons and daughters are not properly guarded. They should never be permitted to go and come when they please, without your knowledge and consent. The unbounded freedom granted to children at this age has proved the ruin of thousands. How many are allowed to be in the streets at night, and parents are content to be ignorant of the associates of their children. Too often companions are chosen whose influence tends only to demoralize. Every son and daughter should be called to account if absent from home at night. Parents should know what company their children are in and at whose house they spend their evenings. Some children deceive their parents with falsehoods to avoid exposure of their wrong course.

Weeds Predominate in an Uncultivated Field: Fathers and mothers too often leave their children to choose for themselves their amusements, their companions, and their occupation. The result is such as might reasonably be expected. Leave a field uncultivated, and it will grow up to thorns and briers. You will never see a lovely flower or a choice shrub peering above the unsightly, poisonous weeds. The worthless bramble will grow luxuriantly without thought or care, while plants that are valued for use or beauty require thorough culture.

Thus it is with our youth. If right habits are formed and right principles established, there is earnest work to be done. If wrong habits are corrected, diligence and perseverance are required to accomplish the task.

Firm but Kind Restraint: The parents should not concede to the inclinations of their children, but should follow the plain path of duty which God has marked out, restraining them in kindness, denying with firmness and determination, yet with love, their wrong desires, and with earnest, prayerful, persevering effort leading their steps away from the world upward to heaven. Children should not be left to drift into whatever way they are inclined, and to go into avenues which are open on every side, leading away from the right path. None are in so great danger as those who apprehend no danger and are impatient of caution and counsel.

Teach Your Children: Children should be trained and educated so that they may calculate to meet with difficulties and expect temptations and dangers. They should be taught to have control over themselves and to nobly overcome difficulties; and if they do not willfully rush into danger and needlessly place themselves in the way of temptation, if they avoid evil influences and vicious society, and then are unavoidably compelled to be in dangerous company, they will have strength of character to stand for the right and preserve principle and will come forth in the strength of God with their morals untainted. The moral powers of youth who have been properly educated, if they make God their trust, will be equal to stand the most powerful test.

RECREATION IS ESSENTIAL

Extreme Views: There are persons with a diseased imagination to whom religion is a tyrant, ruling them as with a rod of iron. Such are constantly mourning over their depravity and groaning over supposed evil. Love does not exist in their hearts; a frown is ever upon their countenances. They are chilled by the innocent laugh from the youth or from anyone. They consider all recreation or amusement a sin and think that the mind must be constantly wrought up to just such a stern, severe pitch. This is one extreme.

Others think that the mind must be ever on the stretch to invent new amusements and diversions in order to gain health. They learn to depend on excitement and are uneasy without it. Such are not true Christians. They go to another extreme. The true principles of Christianity open before all a source of happiness, the height and depth, the length and breadth of which are immeasurable.

To Refresh the Spirits and Invigorate the Body: It is the privilege and duty of Christians to seek to refresh their spirits

174

and invigorate their bodies by innocent recreation, with the purpose of using their physical and mental powers to the glory of God. Our recreations should not be scenes of senseless mirth, taking the form of the nonsensical. We can conduct them in such a manner as will benefit and elevate those with whom we associate, and better qualify us and them to more successfuly attend to the duties devolving upon us as Christians.

Is Essential to Best Work: The time spent in physical exercise is not lost. A proportionate exercise of all the organs and faculties of the body is essential to the best work of each. When the brain is constantly taxed while the other organs of the living machinery are inactive, there is a loss of strength, physical and mental. The physical system is robbed of its healthful tone, the mind loses its freshness and vigor, and a morbid excitability is the result.

Care needs to be exercised in regard to the regulation of hours for sleeping and laboring. We must take periods of rest, periods of recreation, periods for contemplation.

Students Need Relaxation: Those who are engaged in study should have relaxation. The mind must not be constantly confined to close thought, for the delicate mental machinery becomes worn. The body as well as the mind must have exercise.

Office Workers, Too: Few realize the constant, wearing labor of those who are bearing the responsibilities of the work in the office. They are confined within doors day after day and week after week, while a constant strain upon the mental powers is surely undermining their constitutions and lessening their hold on life. They should have a change frequently, should often devote a day wholly to recreation with their families, who are almost entirely deprived of their society. All may not be able to leave the work at the same time; but they should so arrange their work that one or two may go, leaving others to supply their places, and then let these in their turn have the same opportunity.

175

WHAT SHALL WE PLAY?

Substitute the Innocent for the Sinful: Youth cannot be made as sedate and grave as old age, the child as sober as the sire. While sinful amusements are condemned, as they should be, let parents, teachers, and guardians of youth provide in their stead innocent pleasures which will not taint or corrupt the morals. Do not bind down the young to rigid rules and restraints that will lead them to feel themselves oppressed and to break over and rush into paths of folly and destruction. With a firm, kind, considerate hand hold the lines of government, guiding and controlling their minds and purposes, yet so gently, so wisely, so lovingly, that they will still know that you have their best good in view.

While we restrain our children from worldly pleasures that have a tendency to corrupt and mislead, we ought to provide them innocent recreation, to lead them in pleasant paths where there is no danger. No child of God need have a sad or mournful experience. Divine commands, divine promises, show that this is so. Wisdom's ways "are ways of pleasantness, and all her paths are peace."

The Useful Place of the Gymnasium: Gymnastic exercises fill a useful place in many schools, but without careful supervision they are often carried to excess. In the gymnasium many youth, by their attempted feats of strength, have done themselves lifelong injury.

Exercise in a gymnasium, however well conducted, cannot supply the place of recreation in the open air, and for this our schools should afford better opportunity.

When Life Was Less Complex: In early ages, with the people who were under God's direction, life was simple. They lived close to the heart of nature. Their children shared in the labor of the parents and studied the beauties and mysteries of nature's treasure-house. And in the quiet of field and wood they pondered those mighty truths handed down as a sacred trust from generation to generation. Such training produced strong men.

In this age life has become artificial, and men have degenerated. While we may not return fully to the simple habits of those early times, we may learn from them lessons that will make our seasons of recreation what the name implies—seasons of true upbuilding for body and mind and soul.

Family Outings: Let several families living in a city or village unite and leave the occupations which have taxed them physically and mentally, and make an excursion into the country, to the side of a fine lake, or to a nice grove where the scenery of nature is beautiful. They should provide themselves with plain, hygienic food, the very best fruits and grains, and spread their table under the shade of some tree or under the canopy of

177

heaven. The ride, the exercise, and the scenery will quicken the appetite, and they can enjoy a repast which kings might envy.

On such occasions parents and children should feel free from care, labor, and perplexity. Parents should become children with their children, making everything as pleasant for them as possible. Let the whole day be given to recreation. Exercise in the open air for those whose employment has been within doors and sedentary will be beneficial to health. All who can should feel it a duty to pursue this course. Nothing will be lost, but much gained. They can return to their occupations with new life and new courage to engage in their labor with zeal, and they are better prepared to resist disease.

Find Happiness in Nature: Do not think that God wishes us to yield up everything which it is for our happiness here to retain. All He requires us to give up is that which would not be for our good and happiness to retain.

That God who has planted the noble trees and clothed them with their rich foliage, and given us the brilliant and beautiful shades of the flowers, and whose handy and lovely work we see in all the realm of nature, does not design to make us unhappy; He does not design that we shall have no taste and take no pleasure in these things. It is His design that we shall enjoy them. It is His design that we shall be happy in the charms of nature, which are of His own creating.

God's Invitation to Youth: God's invitation comes to each youth, "My son, give Me thine heart; I will keep it pure; I will satisfy its longings with true happiness." God loves to make the youth happy, and that is why He would have them give their hearts into His keeping, that all the God-given faculties of the being may be kept in a vigorous, healthful condition. They are holding God's gift of life. He makes the heart beat; He gives strength to every faculty. Pure enjoyment will not debase one of God's gifts.

DIRECTING JUVENILE RECREATION

Standards Are Being Lowered: Even among Christian parents there has been too much sanctioning of the love of amusements. Parents have received the world's maxim, have conformed to the general opinion that it was necessary that the early life of children and youth should be frittered away in idleness, in selfish amusements, and in foolish indulgences. In

179

this way a taste has been created for exciting pleasure, and children and youth have trained their minds so that they delight in exciting displays; and they have a positive dislike for the sober, useful duties of life. They live lives more after the order of the brute creation. They have no thoughts of God or of eternal realities, but flit like butterflies in their season. They do not act like sensible beings whose lives are capable of measuring with the life of God, and who are accountable to Him for every hour of their time.

Mothers to Invent and Direct Amusements: Instead of sending her children from her presence, that she may not be troubled with their noise and be annoyed with the numerous attentions they would desire, she will feel that her time cannot be better employed than in soothing and diverting their restless, active minds with some amusement or light, happy employment. The mother will be amply repaid for the efforts she may make and the time she may spend to invent amusement for her children.

Young children love society. They cannot, as a general thing, enjoy themselves alone; and the mother should feel that, in most cases, the place for her children when they are in the house is in the room she occupies. She can then have a general oversight of them and be prepared to set little differences right, when appealed to by them, and correct wrong habits or the manifestation of selfishness or passion, and can give their minds a turn in the right direction.

That which children enjoy they think mother can be pleased with, and it is perfectly natural for them to consult mother in little matters of perplexity. And the mother should not wound the heart of her sensitive child by treating the matter with indifference or by refusing to be troubled with such small matters. That which may be small to the mother is large to them. And a word of direction or caution, at the right time, will often prove of great value.

180

Problems of the Perplexing Teen Ages: In the present state of society it is no easy task for parents to restrain their children and instruct them according to the Bible rule of right. Children often become impatient under restraint and wish to have their own way and to go and come as they please.

Especially from the age of ten to eighteen they are inclined to feel that there can be no harm in going to worldly gatherings of young associates. But the experienced Christian parents can see danger. They are acquainted with the peculiar temperaments of their children and know the influence of these things upon their minds; and from a desire for their salvation, they should keep them back from these exciting amusements.

Be Vigilant Especially After Conversion: When the children decide for themselves to leave the pleasures of the world and to become Christ's disciples, what a burden is lifted from the hearts of careful, faithful parents! Yet even then the labors of the parents must not cease. These youth have just commenced in earnest the warfare against sin and against the evils of the natural heart, and they need in a special sense the counsel and watchcare of their parents.

It is the duty of parents to watch the going out and the coming in of their children. They should encourage them and present inducements before them which will attract them at home and lead them to see that their parents are interested for them. They should make home pleasant and cheerful.

THE REWARDS

A Rich Reward Awaits Faithful Parents: If parents give their children the proper education, they themselves will be made happy by seeing the fruit of their careful training in the Christlike character of their children. They are doing God the highest service by presenting to the world well-ordered, well-disciplined families, who not only fear the Lord, but honor and glorify Him by their influence upon other families; and they will receive their reward.

Give your children intellectual culture and moral training. Fortify their young minds with firm, pure principles. While you have opportunity, lay the foundation for a noble manhood and womanhood. Your labor will be rewarded a thousandfold.

If she [the true wife and mother] looks to God for her strength and comfort, and in His wisdom and fear seeks to do her daily duty, she will bind her husband to her heart and see her children coming to maturity honorable men and women, having moral stamina to follow the example of their mother.

The Joys of Heaven Begin in the Home: Heaven and earth are no wider apart today than when shepherds listened to the angels' song. Humanity is still as much the object of heaven's solicitude as when common men of common occupations met angels at noonday and talked with the heavenly messengers in the vineyards and the fields. To us in the common walks of life heaven may be very near. Angels from the courts above will attend the steps of those who come and go at God's command.

The life on earth is the beginning of the life in heaven; education on earth is an initiation into the principles of heaven; the lifework here is a training for the lifework there. What we now are, in character and holy service, is the sure foreshadowing of what we shall be.

Fitted for Heaven: God desires that heaven's plan shall be carried out, and heaven's divine order and harmony prevail, in every family, in every church, in every institution. Did this love leaven society, we should see the outworking of noble principles in Christian refinement and courtesy and in Christian charity toward the purchase of the blood of Christ. Spiritual transformation would be seen in all our families, in our institutions, in our churches. When this transformation takes place, these agencies will become instrumentalities by which God will impart heaven's light to the world and thus, through divine discipline and training, fit men and women for the society of heaven.

The work of wise parents will never be appreciated by the world, but when the judgment shall sit and the books shall be opened, their work will appear as God views it and will be rewarded before men and angels. It will be seen that one child who has been brought up in a faithful way has been a light in the world. It cost tears and anxiety and sleepless nights to oversee the character building of this child, but the work was done wisely, and the parents hear the "Well done" of the Master.

Let the children be taught that as they open their minds to pure, loving thoughts and do loving and helpful deeds, they are clothing themselves with His beautiful garment of character. This apparel will make them beautiful and beloved here and will hereafter be their title of admission to the palace of the King. His promise is:

"They shall walk with me in white: for they are worthy."

THE WORLD TO COME

Eden to Be Restored: The Garden of Eden remained upon the earth long after man had become an outcast from its pleasant paths. The fallen race were long permitted to gaze upon the home of innocence, their entrance barred only by the watching angels. At the cherubim-guarded gate of Paradise the divine glory was revealed. Hither came Adam and his sons to worship God. Here they renewed their vows of obedience to that law the transgression of which had banished them from Eden. When the tide of iniquity overspread the world, and the wickedness of men determined their destruction by a flood of waters, the hand that had planted Eden withdrew it from the earth. But in the final restitution, when there shall be "a new heaven and a new earth," it is to be restored more gloriously adorned than at the beginning.

Then they that have kept God's commandments shall breathe in immortal vigor beneath the tree of life; and through unending ages the inhabitants of sinless worlds shall behold, in that garden of delight, a sample of the perfect work of God's creation, untouched by the curse of sin—a sample of what the whole earth would have become had man but fulfilled the Creator's glorious plan.

The great plan of redemption results in fully bringing back the world into God's favor. All that was lost by sin is restored. Not only man but the earth is redeemed, to be the eternal abode of the obedient. For six thousand years Satan has struggled to maintain possession of the earth. Now God's original purpose in its creation is accomplished. "The saints of the most High shall take the kingdom, and possess the kingdom for ever, even for ever and ever."

The Reward Is Real: A fear of making the future inheritance seem too material has led many to spiritualize away the very truths which lead us to look upon it as our home. Christ assured His disciples that He went to prepare mansions for them in the Father's house. Those who accept the teachings of God's Word will not be wholly ignorant concerning the heavenly abode.

Human language is inadequate to describe the reward of the righteous. It will be known only to those who behold it. No finite mind can comprehend the glory of the Paradise of God.

In the Bible the inheritance of the saved is called a country. There the heavenly Shepherd leads His flock to fountains of living waters. The tree of life yields its fruit every month, and the leaves of the tree are for the service of the nations. There are ever-flowing streams, clear as crystal, and beside them waving trees cast their shadows upon the paths prepared for the ransomed of the Lord. There the widespreading plains swell into hills of beauty, and the mountains of God rear their lofty summits. On those peaceful plains, beside those living streams, God's people, so long pilgrims and wanderers, shall find a home.

There are homes for the pilgrims of earth. There are robes for the righteous, with crowns of glory and palms of victory. All that has perplexed us in the providences of God will in the world to come be made plain. The things hard to be understood

185

will then find explanation. The mysteries of grace will unfold before us. Where our finite minds discovered only confusion and broken promises, we shall see the most perfect and beautiful harmony. We shall know that infinite love ordered the experiences that seemed most trying. As we realize the tender care of Him who makes all things work together for our good, we shall rejoice with joy unspeakable and full of glory.

We are homeward bound. He who loved us so much as to die for us hath builded for us a city. The New Jerusalem is our place of rest. There will be no sadness in the City of God. No wail of sorrow, no dirge of crushed hopes and buried affections, will evermore be heard. Soon the garments of heaviness will be changed for the wedding garment. Soon we shall witness the coronation of our King. Those whose lives have been hidden with Christ, those who on this earth have fought the good fight of faith, will shine forth with the Redeemer's glory in the kingdom of God.

The United Family of Heaven and Earth: There the redeemed shall "know, even as also they are known." The loves and sympathies which God Himself has planted in the soul shall there find truest and sweetest exercise. The pure communion with holy beings, the harmonious social life with the blessed angels and with the faithful ones of all ages who have washed their robes and made them white in the blood of the Lamb, the sacred ties that bind together "the whole family in heaven and earth"—these help to constitute the happiness of the redeemed.

Let all that is beautiful in our earthly home remind us of the crystal river and green fields, the waving trees and the living fountains, the shining city and the white-robed singers, of our heavenly home—that world of beauty which no artist can picture, no mortal tongue describe. "Eye hath not seen, nor ear heard, neither have entered into the heart of man, the things which God hath prepared for them that love him."

PEN PICTURES OF THE NEW EARTH

Learning in the Hereafter: Do you think we shall not learn anything there? We have not the slightest idea of what will then be opened before us. With Christ we shall walk beside the living waters. He will unfold to us the beauty and glory of nature. He will reveal what He is to us and what we are to Him. Truth we cannot know now because of finite limitations, we shall know hereafter.

Heaven is a school; its field of study, the universe; its teacher, the Infinite One. A branch of this school was established in Eden; and, the plan of redemption accomplished, education will again be taken up in the Eden school.

There, when the veil that darkens our vision shall be removed and our eyes shall behold that world of beauty of which we now catch glimpses through the microscope; when we look on the glories of the heavens, now scanned afar through the telescope; when, the blight of sin removed, the whole earth shall appear "in the beauty of the Lord our God," what a field will be open to our study!

Knowledge Will Be Progressive: All the treasures of the universe will be open to the study of God's redeemed. Unfettered by mortality, they wing their tireless flight to worlds afar—worlds that thrilled with sorrow at the spectacle of human woe and rang with songs of gladness at the tidings of a ransomed soul. With unutterable delight the children of earth enter into the joy and the wisdom of unfallen beings. They share the

187

treasures of knowledge and understanding gained through the ages upon ages in contemplation of God's handiwork. With undimmed vision they gaze upon the glory of creation—suns and stars and systems, all in their appointed order circling the throne of Deity. Upon all things, from the least to the greatest, the Creator's name is written, and in all are the riches of His power displayed.

And the years of eternity, as they roll, will bring richer and still more glorious revelations of God and of Christ. As knowledge is progressive, so will love, reverence, and happiness increase. The more men learn of God, the greater will be their admiration of His character.

Occupations in the New Earth: There every power will be developed, every capability increased. The grandest enterprises will be carried forward, the loftiest aspirations will be reached, the highest ambitions realized. And still there will arise new heights to surmount, new wonders to admire, new truths to comprehend, fresh objects to call forth the powers of body and mind and soul.

An Appeal for Personal Preparation: I urge you to prepare for the coming of Christ in the clouds of heaven. Day by day cast the love of the world out of your hearts. Understand by experience what it means to have fellowship with Christ. Prepare for the judgment, that when Christ shall come to be admired in all them that believe, you may be among those who will meet Him in peace.

In that day the redeemed will shine forth in the glory of the Father and the Son. The angels, touching their golden harps, will welcome the King and His trophies of victory—those who have been washed and made white in the blood of the Lamb. A song of triumph shall peal forth, filling all heaven. Christ has conquered. He enters the heavenly courts, accompanied by His redeemed ones, the witnesses that His mission of suffering and sacrifice has not been in vain.